shark life

shark
life

true stories about
sharks & the sea

peter benchley

Adapted for young people by
Karen Wojtyla

delacorte press

Published by
Delacorte Press
an imprint of
Random House Children's Books
a division of Random House, Inc.
New York

Visit us on the Web! www.randomhouse.com/kids
Educators and librarians, for a variety of teaching tools, visit us at
www.randomhouse.com/teachers

Library of Congress Cataloging-in-Publication Data

Wojtyla, Karen.
Shark life / Peter Benchley ; adapted for young people by Karen Wojtyla.
p. cm.
Adaptation of: Shark trouble / Peter Benchley.
ISBN 0-385-73109-4 (trade) — ISBN 0-385-90135-6 (glb)
1. Sharks—Juvenile literature. 2. Shark attacks—Juvenile literature.
3. Dangerous marine animals—Juvenile literature. I. Benchley, Peter.
Shark trouble. II. Title.
QL638.9.W64 2005
597.3—dc22   2004025396

The text of this book is set in 12-point Times.

Book design by Kenny Holcomb

Printed in the United States of America

April 2005

10 9 8 7 6 5 4 3 2 1

BVG

For Christopher—
great traveler, diver, and boon companion

CONTENTS

Preface:
Aliens in the Sea   1

I
1   South Australia, 1974: Swimming with Nightmares   7
2   Jaws   14
3   South Australia, 1974: Part 2   22
4   South Australia, 1974: Part 3   33

II
5   Shark Attacks: A Summer of Hype   39
6   Sharks: How Little We Know   44
7   Six Dangerous Sharks   50
8   Swimming Safely in the Sea   70
9   How to Avoid a Shark Attack   86
10 When Good Dives Go Bad   93
11 You Say You *Want* to Dive with Sharks?   102
12 Some Shark Facts and a Story   112

III
13 Dangerous to Man? Moray Eels, Killer Whales,
    Barracudas, and Other Creatures We Fear   127
14 Even *More* Creatures to Avoid . . . and Respect   168
15 Okay, So What Can We Do?   181

Glossary   191

Preface

Aliens in the Sea

Shark attacks are natural news leaders. They are the perfect showstopping spectacle: blood and guts, horror (ANIMAL SAVAGES HUMAN!), and mystery (INVISIBLE TERROR FROM THE DEEP!), and they are highly videogenic. Even if the camera can't get a shot of shark or victim, it can pan the empty beach and the forbidding ocean, focus on the BEACH CLOSED or DANGER: SHARKS signs, and capture the comments of panicky witnesses.

Shark attacks often dominate the news in the summer. Newspapers, magazines, radio and television news, and talk shows keep count of the incidents of supposed carnage. Experts speculate on the causes and meanings of this assault on humanity.

The truth is that the hysteria is not justified by statistics or other facts. Though shark attacks seemed to occur more frequently as the twentieth century went on, thanks to increases in the numbers of people living by the shore and swimming in the water and to vastly improved communications, they leveled off during the 1990s. Sixty to eighty attacks are reported worldwide each year.

Shark attacks continue to occur. But in the United States homicides or fatal accidents at work are ten times more frequent. And motor-vehicle deaths are over a thousand times more common than shark attacks. As for shark-attack fatalities, well, they're so rare that they're not even on the scale.

I have a lunchpail degree in sharks. What I know about them I've learned not from books so much as on the job—or in the water. All my life I have been fascinated by sharks and have spent more than three decades studying, diving with, and writing about them. I've made documentary films about them and been involved in the feature films and television movies made from my novels about sharks, including *Jaws, The Deep,* and *Beast.*

I've swum with sharks of all species, sizes, and temperaments all over the world, from Australia to Bermuda, South Africa to San Diego, almost always on purpose but sometimes by accident. I've been threatened but never attacked, bumped and shoved but never bitten, and—many times—frightened out of my flippers.

Over the years I've learned how to swim, snorkel, and dive safely in the ocean. I've learned how to exist—coexist, really—with sharks and the hundreds of other marine animals I've been lucky enough to encounter. That's why I've written this book about sharks and other sea creatures, and about understanding how to be safe in the ocean.

In these pages, I pass along what I've learned about

sharks and how to minimize the chances of getting in trouble with them. I also describe how to maximize the chances of seeing sharks, something that is becoming harder and harder to do.

Shark attacks on human beings generate a tremendous amount of media coverage. That's partly because they occur so rarely. But it's also because people are, and always have been, both intrigued and terrified by sharks. Sharks come from one part of the dark castle where our nightmares live— the deep water beyond our sight and understanding. So they stimulate our fears and our fantasies.

For some of us, the fear is a safe fear—a fear of something that is unlikely ever to happen to us.

But for those of us who spend much of our lives in, on, or under the sea, it is a genuine fear, one to be dealt with using knowledge, experience, and judgment.

Of all the shark statistics, one that is almost totally ignored by the media and the public is the most horrible of all: for every human being killed by a shark, roughly ten million sharks are killed by humans. Sometimes they're killed for their skins and their meat. But mostly they're killed for their fins, which are made into soup that is sold for as much as a hundred dollars a bowl all over the world. Shark fin soup is regarded as a delicacy in China and other Asian nations.

Sharks are critical to the ocean's natural balance in ways we know and in ways we are still discovering. Wiping them out, through greed, recklessness, or simple ignorance, would be a tragedy—not just a moral tragedy, but an environmental one as well.

For all we read and hear about "unprovoked" shark attacks, I've come to believe that there's no such thing. We provoke sharks every time we enter the water where they happen to be, for we forget: the ocean is not our territory, it's theirs.

None of us would stroll casually into the Amazon jungle wearing nothing but a bathing suit and carrying a tube of sun cream and a can of bug spray for protection. We know that the jungle is not our natural habitat. We realize we're intruders in the jungle, where many creatures regard us as a threat or as prey. Those creatures will use every mechanism nature has given them—sting, bite, poison, whatever—to ward us off or attack us.

In short, we give the jungle the respect it deserves.

Yet many people regard the ocean casually and don't think about its dangers. Humans need to recognize that we represent a tiny minority on our planet. Seventy percent of the earth is covered by water, leaving to us a mere three square miles out of every ten.

Of our planet's biomass (the grand total of all living things), more than 80 percent inhabits the seas and oceans. All of those creatures have to eat, from the tiniest copepod to the largest carnivorous fish in the world: the great white shark.

And so, when we plunge into the water, we must be aware that *we* are the aliens. We must heed the signs that a shark could be patrolling nearby—signs such as birds working a school of baitfish just offshore, fishermen in small boats with rods bent double and the surface of the water oily with a slick of chum, and other warning signs I'll describe in these pages. We need to realize that when we go into the sea, we are entering hostile territory. We should take at least the basic precautions, knowing that we are fair game to the predators that live there.

I don't mean for a moment that we should stay out of the sea. But we need to prepare ourselves to swim safely in it.

We cannot survive without healthy seas. The sea sustains all life on earth, controlling our climate and atmosphere, generating the air we breathe and the water we drink. Yet only now are we beginning to realize that we have the power to destroy it. For centuries, human beings have treated the sea as an infinite resource and a bottomless dump. Now we are learning that the sea, like everything else on the earth, is finite and fragile.

This book is about understanding the sea in all its beauty, mystery, and power. It is about respecting the sea and its creatures, many of which are exotic, complex, and more intriguing than anything ever imagined by the mind of man.

But mostly, it is about sharks and my experiences with them. Sharks are perfect predators whose form and function have not changed significantly in more than thirty million years. I'll try to pass on what I've learned about sharks and about keeping safe in the sea. I'll try to show you what sharks are like and why they don't want to hurt you or eat you. In fact, sharks would like nothing better than to be left alone to do what nature has programmed them to do: swim, eat, and make little sharks.

I

1
South Australia, 1974
Swimming with Nightmares

Let's start with a story about sharks: Dangerous Reef, in the Neptune Islands, 1974.

Blinded by blood, nauseated by the taste of fish guts, whale oil, and putrid horseflesh, I gripped the aluminum bars of the shark cage. I tried to steady myself against the violent jolts as the cage was tossed by the choppy sea. A couple of feet above me, the surface was a prism that scattered rays of gray from the overcast sky. Below me, the bottom was a dim plain of sand sparsely covered with strands of waving grass.

The water was cold, and my core body heat was dropping; it could no longer warm the icy water seeping into my wet suit. I shivered, and my teeth chattered against the rubber mouthpiece of my regulator.

Happy now? I thought. *Ten thousand miles you flew for the privilege of freezing to death in a sea of stinking chum.*

I imagined the people on the boat overhead, warmed by

sunlight and cups of steaming tea, cozy in their woolen sweaters. My wife, Wendy, was there, and the film crew from ABC-TV's *The American Sportsman*. So were the boat crew and their leader, Rodney Fox, the world's most famous shark-attack survivor.

I thought of the animal I was there to see: the great white shark, largest carnivorous (meat-eating) fish in the sea. Underwater sightings were rare; rarer still were motion pictures of great whites in the wild.

And I thought of *why* I was bobbing alone in a flimsy cage in the frigid sea. I had written a novel about that shark and called it *Jaws*. When it had unexpectedly become a popular success, a television producer had challenged me to go diving with the monster of my imagination. How could I say no? I thought then.

Now, though, I wondered how I could have said yes.

Visibility was poor—ten feet? Twenty? It was impossible to tell because nothing moved in the blue gloom surrounding me. I turned slowly, trying to see in all directions at once. I peered over, under, beside the clouds of blood that billowed vividly against the blue-green water.

I had expected to find silence underwater, but my breath roared like wind in a tunnel as I inhaled through my regulator. My exhales gurgled noisily, like bubbles being blown through a straw in a drink. Waves slapped against the loose-fitting top hatch of the cage, and the joints creaked. When the rope that tied the cage to the boat drew taut, there was a thudding noise and the clank of the steel ring scraping against its anchor plate.

Then I saw movement. Something was moving against the blue. Something dark. It was there and gone and there again. It wasn't coming from the side or circling me. It was coming straight at me, slowly, deliberately, unhurried, emerging from the mist.

I stopped breathing—not intentionally but reflexively, as if by stopping my breath I could stop all movement. I heard my pulse hammering in my ears. I wasn't afraid, exactly. I had been afraid, before, on the boat, but by now I had passed through fear. I was in a state of excitement and something like shocked disbelief.

There it is! Feel the pressure in the water as the body moves through it. The size of it! My God, the size!

The animal kept coming, and now I could see all of it: the pointed snout, the steel gray upper body in stark contrast with the ghostly white belly, the symmetry of the pectoral fins, the awful knife blade of the dorsal fin. The tail fin swung powerfully back and forth, propelling the enormous body toward me. It came slowly, steadily, as if it had no need for speed, for it knew it could not be stopped.

It did not slow, did not hesitate. Its black eyes showed no interest or excitement. As it drew within a few feet of me, it opened its mouth. I saw first the lower jaw, crowded with jagged, needle-pointed teeth; then, as the upper jaw detached from the skull and dropped, the huge, triangular cutting teeth, each side serrated like a saw blade.

The great white's mouth opened wider and wider, until it seemed it would swallow the entire cage, and me within it. I stared into the huge pink and white cavern that narrowed into a black hole, the gullet. I could see rows and rows of spare teeth buried in the gum tissue. Each tooth was a holstered weapon waiting to replace a tooth lost in battle. Far back on each side of the massive head, gill flaps fluttered open and shut, letting in flickering rays of light.

A millisecond before the mouth would have banged into the cage, the great white bit down and was rammed forward by a sudden thrust of its powerful tail. The upper teeth struck four inches from my face. They scraped noisily—horribly—against the aluminum bars. Then the lower teeth gnashed quickly, looking for something solid to sink into.

I shrank back, stumbling, until I could cringe in relative safety in a far corner of the cage.

My brain shouted, *You . . . you of all people ought to know: HUMAN BEINGS DO NOT BELONG IN THE WATER WITH GREAT WHITE SHARKS!*

The shark withdrew, then quickly bit the cage again, and again. It wasn't till the third or fourth bite that I realized the shark wasn't really attacking. It was more like an exploration, a testing. A tasting.

Then the shark turned, showing its flank. I crept forward and reached between the bars to feel its skin. It felt hard and solid, a torpedo of muscle, sleek and polished like steel. I let my fingers trail along with the movement of the animal. But when I rubbed the other way, against the grain, I felt the legendary sandpaper texture. The skin is made of millions upon millions of tiny toothlike particles, the dermal denticles.

The shark was moving away, upward. It had found a hunk of horsemeat, probably ten pounds, possibly twenty, dangling in the chum. The shark's mouth opened and—in a split-second replay of the bite on the cage—it swallowed the chunk of horse whole. Its gullet bulged once as the meat and bone passed through on its way to the gut.

Excited now, the shark turned again in search of something more to eat. It bit randomly, gaping and snapping as if hoping the next bite, or the next, would prove fruitful.

I saw a length of rope drift into its gaping mouth. With a start, I realized it was the lifeline, the only connection between the cage and the boat.

Drift out again. Don't get caught. Not in the mouth. Please.

The great white's mouth closed and opened, closed and opened. The shark shook its head, trying to get rid of the rope. But the rope was stuck.

In a fraction of a second, I saw that the rope had snagged between two—perhaps three or four—of the shark's teeth.

At that instant, the creature's small, primitive brain must have sent a message of alarm, for suddenly the shark seemed to panic. Instinct took over. The animal's tremendous strength and great weight—at least a ton, I knew, spread over its fourteen-foot length—exploded in frenzied thrashing.

The shark's tail whipped one way and its head the other. Its body slammed against the cage, against the boat, from the cage to the boat. I was upside down, then on my side, then bashed against the side of the boat. Finally there was no up and no down for me, only a burst of bubbles amid a cloud of blood and shreds of flesh from the chum and the butchered horse.

What are they doing up there? Don't they see what's going on? Why doesn't somebody do something?

For a second I saw the shark's head and the rope that had disappeared into its mouth—and that's the last thing I remember seeing for a long, long time. For when the shark's tail bashed the cage again, the cage slid down and swung into the darkness beneath the boat.

I knew what would happen next. I had heard of it happening once before: the shark's teeth would sever the rope. My survival would depend on precisely where the rope was severed. If the shark found itself free of the cage, it would flee, leaving the cage to drift away and, perhaps, sink. Someone from the boat would get a line to me. Eventually.

But if the rope stayed caught in the shark's mouth, the

animal might drag the cage to the bottom, fifty feet away, and beat it to pieces. If I was going to survive, I would have to find the rope, grab it, and cut it, all while being tumbled about like dice in a cup.

I reached for the knife in the rubber sheath strapped to my leg.

This isn't really happening. It can't be! I'm just a writer! I write fiction!

It was happening, though. And even in all that chaos, I appreciated the irony.

How many other writers, I wondered, *have written the story that foretells their own horrible death?*

2

Jaws

I began to think about writing *Jaws* in the early 1970s. I remember phoning my father, Nathaniel, one day in Nantucket, where he lived year-round. He was a novelist, playwright, screenwriter, and author of children's books. His best-known novel was a wonderful story called *The Off-Islanders,* which was made into the movie *The Russians Are Coming! The Russians Are Coming!* His books for kids included *Sam the Minuteman* and *Red Fox and His Canoe.* He had spent four years in the navy during World War II and was very knowledgeable about the sea.

"What would happen," I asked him, "if you cut a body in two? What would float? Any of it?"

"Depends where you cut it," he said. "Cut it above the air sacs, the lower half will float. Cut it below the air sacs, the upper half will float." He paused, then asked, "What're you up to?"

"Trying to tell a story about a shark."

"That's some shark."

"Yup," I said. "I don't imagine anything'll come of it, but I figure, why not?"

"Sure. Nothing to lose."

What I was doing, in fact, was making one final attempt to stay alive as a writer. I was scratching out a few days' work each week from a division of *Newsweek*, and I was writing articles, on anything, for anyone who would pay for them. I wrote book reviews, movie reviews, travel pieces, and—most enjoyably—reports from Nantucket, Bermuda, and New Zealand for *National Geographic* magazine.

I tried to save a couple of days each week for work of my own. The results were mostly short stories and film scripts that didn't sell. Since there was no room to work at home and I couldn't afford a proper office, I rented an empty back room in a furnace supply company. The manufacture and repair of furnaces isn't the quietest of businesses, and it wasn't a great place for the flowering of the creative imagination. But since the garden of my imagination appeared to be producing only weeds, little seemed to be lost to the music of sledgehammers against sheet metal.

I was very lucky to have a literary agent. As a favor to my father, one of his agents, a kindly and generous woman named Roberta Pryor, had taken me on when I was sixteen. She had even sold a short story of mine when I was twenty. Roberta refused to give up on me and encouraged me to have lunch with editors from publishing houses. I kept two ideas ready for those lunches. One idea was for a nonfiction book, a history of pirates, who had always interested me. The other was for a fictional book about a great white shark that terrorizes a resort community. Folded in my wallet was a yellowed 1964 clipping from the *New York Daily News* that reported the capture of a 4,550-pound great white shark off Long Island. I would show it at the first hint of disbelief that such an animal could exist, let alone that it might attack boats and eat people.

I believe that everyone on earth is, at some period in his or her life, fascinated by sharks or dinosaurs or both. Most of us outgrow our obsession. A lucky few are able to indulge it throughout our lives. When I was a boy, I spent my summers on the island of Nantucket, whose waters were well populated by sharks: sand sharks, blue sharks, and, once in a great while, a mako. I fished frequently, and on hot and windless days the Atlantic Ocean surrounding Nantucket sprouted shark fins like asparagus spears. To me they spoke of the unknown, the mysterious, of menace and adventure—and (when I'd get carried away) of ancient evil.

I had read most of the available literature about sharks—there wasn't much. I had seen *Blue Water, White Death,* the 1971 feature film that, for me, remains the finest documentary ever made about sharks. So I knew as much as any amateur about sharks. Editors went away from our meetings interested and armed with a vague pledge from me to write an outline—sometime, about something to do with sharks—and I went away and didn't write the outline.

Then one day I had lunch with Tom Congdon, an editor at Doubleday, and when he returned to his office, he called Roberta and offered to pay me one thousand dollars for the first four chapters of an untitled shark novel. That one thousand dollars would be part of an overall advance of seventy-five hundred dollars, which would be paid when—and if—I delivered a complete and acceptable manuscript.

Of course, I fell headfirst into the trap. I signed the paper, took the money, and cashed the check. I didn't write the four chapters until Roberta told me I'd have to either write them or return the money (which, naturally, had vanished). Then I did write the four chapters, and Tom didn't like them because I had tried to write them funny. (Writing a funny thriller about a shark eating people is, I soon realized, nearly impossible.) I rewrote the pages, and Tom liked them. So I continued with the story, which did, at last, get done, after more than a year of writing and rewriting.

There was a problem with the title: we didn't have one. Half an hour before the book was to go into production, there was still no title. Tom and I reviewed some of the hundred plus titles we had tried. I had come up with titles like *A Stillness in the Water* and *The Silence of Death*. There were monster titles: *Leviathan, Leviathan Rising, The Jaws of Leviathan*. There were *White Death* and *The Jaws of Death* and *Summer of the Shark*. My father contributed *Wha's That Noshin' on My Laig?*

Finally I said, "Look, there's no way we're gonna agree

on a title. There's only one word we both like, so let's make that the title. Let's call it *Jaws.*"

Tom thought for a moment, then nodded. "At least it's short."

I called my father and told him the title.

"What's it mean?" he asked.

"I have no idea," I said. "But at least it's short."

I called Roberta and told her the title. "That's terrible," she said. "What's it mean?"

"Beats me," I replied. "But it sure is short."

Though no one liked it much, no one had a better idea, so no one protested. After all, they reasoned, what we have here is a first novel, and nobody reads first novels, anyway. Besides, it's a first novel about a fish, for God's sake, and who cares? At least it's done.

Furthermore, we all loudly agreed that there wasn't a chance that anybody would ever make a movie out of the book. I knew it was impossible to catch and train a great white shark. Everybody else knew that Hollywood's special-effects technology was nowhere near sophisticated enough to make a believable model of a great white shark.

So we called it *Jaws,* and that, for the time being, was that.

✛ ✛ ✛ ✛

The book was published in the spring of 1974, to generally good reviews. *Jaws* was not, in hardcover, the huge bestseller that legend has made it. It climbed slowly up the list of the *New York Times Book Review,* and though it lingered for forty-four weeks, it never made it to number one. An obstinate book about a rabbit, *Watership Down,* refused to give up the number one slot. Nor did *Jaws* sell anywhere near the number of hardcover copies a bestseller would today. Nowadays, novels like J. K. Rowling's Harry Potter books sell millions of copies. *Jaws* sold about 125,000 copies.

The story in paperback was entirely different. *Jaws* was number one for months on lists all over the world. In the United States alone it sold more than nine million copies. But that success had to do in part with the release of the movie.

Film rights to *Jaws* had been bought by Universal Pictures. They permitted me to write a couple of the early drafts of the screenplay, and—knowing that in the heart of many writers lives a secret ham—they actually cast me in the film. The movie went into production not long after the book was published. I visited the set, played the role of the TV reporter on the beach on the Fourth of July, and, meanwhile, tried unsuccessfully to live a normal life.

Sometime during that hectic spring and summer of 1974, John Wilcox, producer of ABC's television show *The American Sportsman,* contacted me. He wanted to know if I'd be interested in traveling to Australia to do a show about going into the water (in a cage, of course) with great white sharks. *The American Sportsman,* which ran for twenty years, from 1966 to 1986, was among the first and best of the TV sports shows. Each week it ran three or four segments that featured celebrities participating in an outdoor sport. Thus far, Wilcox hadn't produced any scuba-diving segments because there hadn't been any demand for them. Where was the excitement or entertainment in taking a movie camera underwater, where the celebrity couldn't talk, and filming fish swimming around on a reef?

Jaws and all the attention it was getting led Wilcox to believe that sharks—unseen, dangerous, and, best of all, man-eating—could produce . . . well, I have to say it . . . monster ratings.

I was a certified diver, though by no means a confidently experienced one. Years earlier, while earning my certification in the Bahamas, I had seen a shark in the distance, minding its own business. My reaction had been a common one: I panicked. I grabbed my instructor by the arm, pointed at the shark, and gestured that it was time for us to surface. When he calmly refused, I breathed so deeply and so rapidly that I sucked my tank dry.

Yet I agreed to journey to Australia for ABC—on one condition: I wanted to bring with me one of the handful of people who had ever been in the water with white sharks: Stan Waterman. Stan was a cameraman and an associate producer on *Blue Water, White Death* and a pioneer in scuba diving. Most important, Stan was a neighbor and close friend whom I would trust with my life.

It sounded like fun. After spending the previous year and a half locked up in a room alone, writing, I thought it would be a welcome relief, an adventure. As with the writing and publishing of *Jaws* and the writing, shooting, and subsequent release of the movie, I hadn't the faintest idea what I was about to get myself into.

3
South Australia, 1974
Part 2

The journey for *The American Sportsman* had not begun in that cage in the home range of the great white sharks: the cold, dark waters near Dangerous Reef in the Neptune Islands. Rather, the shooting schedule had been designed, wisely, to introduce me gradually to diving with sharks in the wild. The TV crew wanted me to get used to seeing sharks underwater. They hoped I would learn from swimming with some of the less imposing species that while sharks are indeed powerful and efficient predators, they know that human beings are not desirable prey.

No one—I least of all—wanted me to be so frightened that I'd refuse to participate in the "money shots." Those were the moments of peril with great white sharks that TV viewers would tune in to see. In the past, some celebrities had frozen at critical moments and refused to go on. Sometimes they invented elaborate excuses that included suddenly being called to meetings with Hollywood moguls. Somehow these calls had mysteriously made their way to places so remote that they were unreachable by phone, wires, or radio. (There were no faxes back then, no cell phones, no satellite dishes, no pagers.)

We began on the Great Barrier Reef, where there was no danger of seeing a great white shark because, supposedly, great whites didn't exist on the Barrier Reef. The water there was considered too warm; white sharks preferred the cool seas of South Australia (and California, New York, and Massachusetts). Also, the Barrier Reef was well charted, well known, and visited year-round by thousands of divers. The ports along the East Coast were populated by knowledgeable seamen who could choose specific parts of the reef to dive in, depending on what the clients wanted to see.

The Great Barrier Reef is one of our planet's largest living organisms, an interconnected complex of creatures that is fifteen hundred miles long. It's the longest, the biggest, the richest reef system in the world. It has wild areas, restricted areas, populated areas, tourist areas, and conservation areas.

It was decided that I should learn how to dive with sharks by beginning with what Australians call bronze whalers. Bronze whalers are relatively small sharks (five to seven feet long) that tend to gather in schools. They are generally regarded as controllable by people experienced in dealing with them, although they can be dangerous when their territory is threatened or when they're fighting over food.

Our first morning on the reef, Stan Waterman had assembled the underwater housing for his 16mm movie camera. He had decided to take the empty housing into the water first, to make sure it wouldn't spring a leak and flood his camera with salt water.

He strapped on a scuba tank and I followed him, eager to get as much experience as possible under safe conditions (as I had been assured they were). We sat on the swim step at the back of the boat—the gaudy reef and sandy bottom were clearly visible through no more than thirty feet of clear water—rinsed our masks, and rolled forward into the sea.

The first couple of seconds of every dive are discombobulating. When you're surrounded by bubbles escaping from your regulator and your equipment, you're blind and deaf. Up feels like down, down like up. Very quickly, though, your eyes adjust, and your inner ear orients you in this new space. You hear the comforting sound of air being inhaled and exhaled through your regulator.

When we regained our senses, Stan and I nodded to each other and started down.

He saw it first and recognized it immediately. I might have seen it, too; I don't remember. But I do remember noticing its peculiar features: the pointed snout, the blue-gray upper body and stark white underbelly, the perfect triangle of pectoral fins and dorsal fin. And one of the dead giveaways I would soon learn to recognize: the apparently toothless upper jaw, lip rolled under, concealing the rows of sheathed daggers.

It was angling up toward us, slowly, as if idly curious.

Stan touched my arm and looked into my eyes. There was something so earnest in his gaze—the eyes that normally shone and sparkled were as flat as slate—that I knew instantly what he was saying: Stick with me, do what I do, for we are being approached by a Great . . . White . . . Shark.

My first instinct, of course, was to turn and flee, but by now the shark was within ten or fifteen feet of us. Even in my terror I knew that flight would send a one-word message to the animal: food. So I followed Stan.

Holding his camera housing before him, Stan swam slowly down, directly toward the shark. I could see that this was not, in fact, a big great white, though part of my brain registered it as the size of a rhinoceros. It was about ten feet long, a young male. It was probably still adapting to its world, learning about water temperature, hunting grounds, feeding methods—and now, analyzing prey.

I found myself wondering what we looked like to the shark. Large, loud, bubbling creatures, similar to seals or sea lions in our black wet suits, but with one big difference: we were unafraid (after all, we weren't running but were actually approaching). We might even look aggressive. Still, nothing to be feared. The only things this animal would fear would be larger versions of itself and killer whales.

Quietly, we descended. Even more quietly, it ascended.

Are you crazy? Why are you playing chicken with a great white shark?

When we were no more than five feet apart, the shark blinked. Without seeming to flick its tail or alter the pitch of its fins or move a muscle, it changed direction from up to down and passed beneath us. We stopped and turned, and watched the shark disappear into the gray canyons of the deeper reef.

Once safe back aboard the boat, I protested. "I thought . . . you said . . . you promised . . ."

"I know," Stan said with a grin. "Amazing, isn't it? Can you believe the luck? And I didn't even have my camera!"

"But what about—"

"The first law of sharks," he said, "is this: forget all the laws about sharks."

For the next nine days we waited and watched and baited and dove—day and night, hour after hour—and we saw no sharks of any species. We set out chum slicks of fish guts and oil; the crew speared fish and we hung the corpses off the stern of the boat. We prepared savory baits and tied them to brain corals and then hid quietly in crannies in the reef until, one by one, we ran out of air and surfaced. Then we put new tanks into our backpacks and descended again to resume our posts.

We swam free, without cages. Back then most divers thought you needed cages only when you were dealing with great white sharks, or when you were filming large numbers of big sharks that might be aggressive. Now we know better.

The water was warmer than eighty degrees, and our wet suits kept us comfortable for a long time. But eventually the hardiest of us got chilly and began to shiver, and, again one by one, we gave in to the cold and surfaced for good.

With one day to go in this first half of our schedule, we had no film, not a single frame of any shark in the water, with or without people. None of the experts could *imagine* where the sharks could possibly have gone. Bronze whalers were *always* around this area. The local crew had been here, all told, for more than fifty years, and they had never seen anything like this. If only we'd been here two weeks before; the sharks had been jumping everywhere. And so on—every excuse ever uttered by every fishing guide and boat captain who has ever struck a dry hole in the ocean.

Our tenth and last day began exactly like the others: clear, hot, flat calm, no breeze, and very little current. The corpse of a big stingray was tied to a brain coral as bait. I dove down and took my position in the sand. I was kneeling (as instructed) exactly thirty-one inches from the stingray. This was the distance needed for Stan to capture, in the same picture frame, me and any shark that might show up.

After about an hour I had emptied my tank of compressed air. So I surfaced, stretched, warmed myself in the sun for a few minutes, changed tanks, and dove down again.

Almost weightless, rocked gently by what current there was, snug and cozy in my rubber suit in the warm ocean, I fell asleep. At least, I must have, for I have no memory of time passing or of seeing or hearing anything until I felt Stan tap my shoulder. I opened my eyes and saw, less than an arm's length away, a shark the size of a school bus about to assault our stingray bait.

It was a tiger shark. There was no mistaking the stripes on its flanks, the peculiar catfish-like protrusions from its nasal passages, the broad, flat head, and the curved, serrated teeth in its top and bottom jaws. A tiger is one of the few species of shark that has well earned the title man-eater. Its mouth was open, and the upper jaw had dropped down and rolled its teeth into the bite position.

The nictitating membrane—a defense mechanism in many sharks designed to cover the eyeball and protect it from the claws or teeth of struggling prey—had slid up and over all but a tiny slit of the yellowish eye. That was a sign that the shark had decided to bite—had, in fact, begun to bite. I thought the tiger looked like a maniac.

Startled as much as afraid, I must have flinched backward, for I felt Stan's hand pushing me forward.

Thirty-one inches, I thought. *That thing is thirty-one inches from my face.*

The tiger shark was enormous, at least thirteen feet long. It grabbed the stingray and began to shake it. The huge body writhed, stirring up a cloud of sand and generating pressure waves that rocked me backward. I looked for something to hold on to, to steady myself. But the only solid structure within reach was the brain coral to which the ray was tied. Somehow I thought that to put my hands into the shark's mouth might be . . . a bad idea.

The shark's teeth sawed off one wing of the stingray. Then, swallowing, it swam away, swinging in a slow circle to approach the bait again.

As the cloud of sand cleared and settled, movement somewhere above made me look up. Halfway to the surface, perhaps fifteen feet away, was a second tiger shark, this one as big as a midsize sedan. It was swimming with agitated movements, and it looked angry.

I knew why it was frustrated. In the world of tiger sharks—and several other species—the biggest feeds first. This smaller animal, which we decided later was about eleven feet long, had no choice but to watch as the tasty meal was consumed by the larger fellow.

Again the big tiger bit down on the stingray, seeming this time to take the entire brain coral in its mouth. Its teeth tore the carcass to pieces. Shreds of gray-black skin flew out through the shark's gill slits and sank to the sand. Tiny fish snatched them up and retreated to eat them in the shelter of the reef.

I was paralyzed, not from fear but from fascination and concentration. And then—

Oh, no.

I couldn't breathe. Trying to inhale was like sucking on an empty Coke bottle. Quickly I looked at my air gauge: zero.

I was out of air.

For once I didn't panic, and I didn't shoot for the surface. I knew the risk of an air embolism. If you ascend too fast, holding your breath, the air in your lungs will expand and blow a hole in a lung. Then an air bubble can travel to your heart or brain and kill or cripple you. If I was going to try a free ascent, I wanted to do it properly: drop my weights, open my mouth, and exhale constantly as I swam for the surface.

But I also knew that there was, in fact, at least one more breath of air in the tank, though I'd have to ascend to get it. Air that has compressed as a diver descends expands when he ascends. Unless you have truly sucked a vacuum into your tank, chances are there's a bit of crucial, life-sustaining air left.

Of course, to be on the surface above two tiger sharks, one feeding and one angry because it couldn't feed, was not an ideal situation. Still, it struck me as preferable to drowning. Besides, I didn't intend to stay on the surface for long. I looked up and saw the boat above me. If I went up at the right angle, I should be able to surface near—if not exactly at—the dive step on the boat.

I turned to Stan and made the out-of-air signal—a finger

drawn across the throat. Then I rose off the sand bottom, slowly, as quietly as possible. I straightened my legs for the first time in more than an hour and started to kick.

Both legs cramped at the same time and in exactly the same way: my hamstrings sprang taut, snapping each leg up under my body. That left me with useless legs, feet, and fins. The sudden pain made me gasp . . . except there was no air to gasp.

Now you are in trouble. . . . What to do, what to do, what to do?

I pulled the release on my weight belt. Twenty-five pounds of lead dropped from my waist, so immediately I began to rise.

A breath of air became available, and I gulped it down. I was careful to leave my mouth open to let my exhaling breath escape.

The last thing I saw before my head popped through the surface was the second tiger shark, swimming in circles beneath me. Alerted by my noisy ascent, it had swum over to see what was going on. Its body was tilted slightly, so that I could see its eye watching me.

No worries, mate, I thought. *Just put an arm out and let 'em pull you aboard the boat.*

Frightened and disoriented by the pain in my locked legs, I extended an arm and . . . nothing. Nobody grabbed it.

I spun in place, and . . . *Well, no wonder.* The boat was

ten yards away and drifting farther. *No! Impossible!* The boat was anchored. . . . I was the one drifting. I was caught in a surface current and being swept away.

I raised my arms, hoping to communicate that I was helpless in the water. Somehow that message got through to our director, Scott Ransom. He grabbed a rope, flung himself off the stern of the boat, and swam to me. Together we held on to the rope, and the crew pulled us to the boat.

I never once looked down. If the tiger shark was pursuing us, I didn't want to know.

Thus ended the "easy" part of the shoot, the get-acquainted-with-sharks part. From here on, I knew, matters would become serious. We were headed south, to Dangerous Reef. There I would climb into a flimsy cage bobbing in a sea of blood, and a crew of experts would do their best to get a great white shark to approach the cage and try to eat me.

Why? I wondered. *Why did I have to write a novel about a shark? Why not a novel about . . . I don't know . . . a puppy?*

4
South Australia, 1974
Part 3

We flew to Adelaide, South Australia, and from there across Spencer Gulf to Port Lincoln. Port Lincoln was a rugged frontier town in an area full of places with names like Coffin Bay and—our destination—Dangerous Reef.

This was the world of the great white shark. It was also the home of Rodney Fox, a national hero in Australia. Fox had introduced the crew of the movie *Blue Water, White Death* to the great whites of South Australia. He was a shark expert, a tour guide, and a conservationist. Even back then, Rodney knew ten times more than anyone else about great whites. He was the only person in the world who knew how to attract them and film them, underwater, in relative safety.

It was Rodney who had built the cages, chartered the boats, hired the crews, and bought the dead horse to use as bait. It was Rodney who had convinced me that I would be perfectly safe in the cage. The same cage that was now being hammered to rubble by two thousand–plus pounds of pan-icked and enraged great white shark.

As I was slammed about in the cage, I imagined myself reduced from a suddenly successful writer to a surf 'n' turf snack for a prehistoric monster.

The curious thing was that not only was I not afraid, but I *knew* I wasn't afraid. In all the turmoil, violence, confusion, and darkness, my brain made room for a conscious observa-tion about itself. We had departed the realm of fear, my brain and I, and emerged into a peaceful pocket of detached obser-vation. I felt no pain, except for the odd ache when my insu-lated bones thunked against the bars. I watched my stubby rubber fingers plucking uselessly at the little rubber ring that held my knife in its sheath. Every movement looked slow and deliberate, as if the Play mechanism in my mental VCR had been slowed to Frame Advance.

The noise was loud, but each sound was distinct and sur-prising. There was the hollow, metallic whang of the cage slamming against the hull of the boat; the whoosh as a ton of shark flesh lashed wildly through the water; the bubbles blasting both from me and from the rippling gill slits of the huge frightened animal. And, so far in the distance that they might have been imaginary, the shrill sounds of human voices.

The cage began to move, scraping along the bottom of the boat. Now there was light enough for me to see that we—the shark, the cage, and I—were somehow still connected to the boat above. With a thrust of its tail, the giant body lunged upward and forward.

What's this? Now it wants to board the boat?

Suddenly, with swiftness and grace and in complete silence, the shark slid backward and down. It turned and swam away. The rope had disappeared from its mouth. I had a final glimpse of its tail, and then the shark was gone, absorbed into the misty blue sea.

The cage righted itself, but because one of its floating tanks had been punctured, it hung askew. Someone above pulled on the rope, and I felt myself moving up toward the light. Through the moving glassy plane of the surface I saw faces, grotesquely distorted, staring down at me from the boat. In their center was the round black eye of the ABC Sports camera lens.

Once on board, I described my ordeal for the camera, nearly weeping with relief.

Rodney, who had been through infinitely worse experiences, was full of compliments like "You're mad!"

Stan, who had a way with words, said, "Tell me, sir, is it true that you don't know the very meaning of fear?"

Then I described what I thought had gone wrong and asked what had, in fact, happened. There was an awkward pause. Most of the crew seemed unaware that anything had gone wrong. Those few who did know did not seem eager to discuss the matter.

I looked up at the flying bridge, where my wife, Wendy,

was leaning on the railing and watching us with wry amusement. From her expression I could tell immediately that she knew everything, from exactly what had gone wrong to who and what had been involved in correcting it. I was sure that whatever had happened, she had played a role in its satisfactory outcome.

As indeed she had.

In 1974 it was rare for a wife to accompany her husband on an expedition like ours, living in close quarters on small boats. Wendy found herself treated with profound awkwardness, though not with disrespect. When I climbed into the cage and the white shark appeared, Wendy was banished from the action, exiled up to the flying bridge.

She didn't argue, and almost immediately she discovered that she had the best position on the boat. She could see everything that was going on. She watched the giant shark lunging at the baits, bumping and biting the two cages—mine and Stan's. She saw the surface cameramen struggling to keep up with fast-moving figures, shifting light, and splashes of blood and oil and water.

She saw the rope attached to my cage slip into the shark's mouth. She saw it catch between the teeth. She saw the shark growing desperate to rid itself of the cage, thrashing and gnashing and pummeling both cages.

She also saw that nobody else had noticed any of it. They were all too focused on their own tasks. Cameramen were trying for close-ups. Assistants were holding on to the cameramen's belts to keep them from tumbling overboard. Some crewmen were busy ladling more chum into the water. Others could do nothing but stare, openmouthed, as a fish the size of a Buick went berserk behind the boat.

Wendy knew what would happen if the shark couldn't shake loose of the rope. And it soon became obvious that it couldn't.

She slid quickly down the ladder from the flying bridge, marched aft, and pushed aside one chummer and one idle gaper. She took hold of the rope a foot or two behind the cleat to which it was tied on the stern. She leaned over, trying to see the head of the shark and locate the spot where the rope entered its mouth.

Just then the shark raised its head and lunged upward, and Wendy found herself nose to nose with—perhaps twenty-four inches away from—the most notorious, hideous, frightening face in nature. The snout was smeared with red. Bits of flesh clung to its jaws, and blood drooled from the sides of its mouth. The upper jaw was down, in bite position, and gnashing as if trying to climb the rope. The eyes, as big as baseballs, were rolled backward in their sockets—great whites do not have nictitating membranes. As the great body shook, it forced air through its gill slits, making a noise like a grunting pig.

All this Wendy recalled in detail. She also recalled shaking the rope and yelling at the shark. She cursed and called it names she wasn't aware she knew, and demanded that it let go of the rope. The shark grunted at her and twisted its head, showing her one of its ghastly black eyeballs, and the rope sprang free.

The great white slid backward off the stern and away from the boat. When it was fully in the water, it rolled onto its side and, like a fighter plane peeling away from a formation, glided down and away into the darkness.

II

5
Shark Attacks
A Summer of Hype

Every once in a while, shark attacks grip the public imagination. That was what happened in the summer of 2001. Shark attacks dominated the news. Everywhere—on TV, the radio, the Internet—there were stories about "killer" sharks. Early the next year I contacted George Burgess, director of the International Shark Attack File at the University of Florida, and requested the figures for 2001.

Worldwide, the number of shark attacks recorded in 2001 was seventy-six, down from eighty-five the year before.

In the United States, fifty-five people were attacked by sharks in 2001, exactly one more than in 2000. As for fatalities, five people in the world died from shark bites in 2001, twelve in 2000.

"2001 was an average year by U.S. standards, and below average internationally," said Mr. Burgess. "Most important, serious attacks were way down."

Why, then, the shark hysteria?

First of all, human beings look at sharks with both fear and fascination. I think that fascination accounts for the long life *Jaws* has enjoyed as a movie. Aside from the many merits of the Steven Spielberg film, the story apparently touches a deep nerve in a great many people.

There was also the fact that in the summer of 2001, the United States and the world were in a relatively slow news cycle. Not much was going on that was newsworthy.

Then, at dusk on July 6, eight-year-old Jesse Arbogast was attacked by a bull shark in shallow water off Pensacola, Florida. The attack was particularly gruesome and sensational. Somehow, his uncle wrestled the seven-foot shark to shore. He and a park ranger retrieved Jesse's severed arm from the mouth of the shark and rushed it to a hospital, where it was reattached to Jesse. Miraculously, the boy survived.

After that incident, the antennae of the media and the public were set to receive reports of other shark attacks as soon as they happened. And happen they did—the few normal encounters between bathers or surfers and sharks that occur off beaches from New Jersey to Florida.

Each incident was treated as a new sensation. Very soon a trend was declared, and the world was gripped by shark fever.

The fever took hold so strongly partly because of the major changes over the past few years in the way news is broadcast around the world. With the Internet, cable television, cell phones, and satellites, we learn about everything that happens anywhere almost instantly. We also learn about everything that is rumored to have happened anywhere—whether it is true or not.

Here's an example of how quickly rumors can spread and how stories can get exaggerated. On August 14, 2001, a school of sharks was sighted close to shore near St. Petersburg, Florida. No one knew how many sharks there were. The first reports—by telephone and e-mail—described them as "a bunch." Soon there were "dozens," then "hundreds." By the time a reporter for the *St. Petersburg Times* was assigned to cover the story, the number of sharks was "in the thousands."

The suspicious reporter chartered a small plane and flew out over the scene. He didn't know what to expect. Surely there would be too many sharks to count, but would they be moving toward the beaches or away from them? Were the sharks chasing food or hunting for food? Was this mass gathering a breeding event . . . or a killing event?

I spoke to the reporter on the phone after he returned.

"The water was murky," he said, "but I could still count the sharks 'cause it was calm and they were all on or near the surface. There were forty sharks. Exactly forty. Even I could see what they were—blacktips—and they were following a school of baitfish, which happens every day. There were more fishing boats out there than sharks, all intent on killing the 'killers.' It was ridiculous."

By the end of July 2001, shark attacks were being reported almost daily—in Florida, North Carolina, Virginia, all up and down the coast. Most of the "attacks" were incidents that, in a normal year, would not have been reported beyond the local press. But this was not a normal year. The season had been called the Summer of the Shark by *Time* magazine.

The actual number of incidents that summer was not abnormal. There had not, as of that August, been a single shark-attack fatality in U.S. waters. But it seemed to the public that the world (or at least the ocean) had gone crazy.

So-called experts popped up everywhere to offer explanations. Here are some of the reasons they gave for a rise in shark attacks that didn't really exist:

✛ The general decline in fish stocks had left sharks desperate for food; consequently, they were attacking humans. There's no evidence at all to support this theory.

✛ Restrictions imposed by the federal government on shark fishing had created an overabundance of sharks, which were now preying on helpless swimmers. In fact, all the accepted evidence points to a drastic decline in the numbers of nearly every species of shark.

✛ By targeting certain species and ignoring others, commercial fishermen had encouraged a population explosion among bull sharks, which were the villains in several serious attacks. There is simply no evidence of an increase in the bull shark population.

✢ Shark-feeding enterprises, which abound in Florida and elsewhere as tourist attractions, had conditioned sharks to associate the presence of humans with the promise of food. When those sharks encountered people who didn't feed them—for example, swimmers and surfers—they went after the people. This theory is completely unsupported by reliable data.

The "shark summer" of 2001, which had begun on July 6 with the attack on Jesse Arbogast, ended on Labor Day weekend with two fatal attacks—the only two of the summer in the United States.

On Saturday, September 1, ten-year-old David Peltier bled to death after being bitten on the leg while surfing in the waters off Virginia Beach. Two days later Sergei Zaloukaev, twenty-seven, was killed by a shark while he and his wife, Natalia, were wading in the surf off Avon, North Carolina. Natalia was bitten, too, and lost a foot, but she survived.

The summer ended. Then came the horror of September 11. People had a real crisis to worry about, and shark attacks disappeared from the news. In fact, nothing really crazy happened in the oceans that summer. It happened in the media, where a hunger for news stories created a feeding frenzy and a summer of hype.

6
Sharks
How Little We Know

There are a great many sharks, and a great many kinds of sharks, in the sea. Very few—a tiny, insignificant number—will ever have contact with a human being, let alone bother one . . . let alone eat one. As a general rule, being attacked by a shark is not something you should worry about—unless you're a person who worries about being struck by lightning or attacked by killer bees, both of which are more likely to happen to you than a shark attack.

Still, there are actions you can take to reduce the odds even further—besides staying out of the water altogether. There are even one or two things you can do to protect yourself if, God forbid, you ever are attacked by a shark. More about both later.

Each of the following statements about sharks has been printed, reprinted, and guaranteed to be the absolute truth. Of the three, which one would you say is true?

1. Of the 380 species of sharks known to science, fewer than a dozen pose any threat whatever to human beings.

2. Of the more than 400 species of sharks in the world, only 11 have ever been known to attack a human being.

3. Of the 450 species of sharks on record, only 3 qualify as man-eaters.

Don't bother to guess—it's a trick question. The answer is: none of the above. To begin with, nobody knows for certain how many species of sharks there are. Scientists can't agree on how many different species have been discovered and cataloged. Some sharks go by different names in different countries. Australia's gray nurse shark, for example, bears no resemblance to the nurse sharks of the Atlantic and the Caribbean. In some countries, some subspecies are identified as separate species. Most scientists believe that the Zambezi shark and the Lake Nicaragua shark are both bull sharks; a few disagree. Some experts insist that *Carcharodon megalodon,* the fifty-foot monster that roamed the seas thirty million years ago, is a direct ancestor of today's great white shark. Other experts insist that today's makos are the true descendants of *C. megalodon.*

Another reason we don't know precisely how many species of sharks there are is that new sharks—new to humans, that is—are still being discovered. In 1976 a behemoth almost unknown to science, nearly fifteen feet long and weighing three-quarters of a ton, was caught accidentally by a U.S. Navy ship off Hawaii. A plankton feeder with an enormous mouth, it was dubbed megamouth. A dozen other specimens have since turned up, everywhere from Japan to Brazil. In 1990 one was filmed swimming free, after it had been released from the net that had caught it off California. For all its size and heft, megamouth is slow, curious, and not at all aggressive.

More new species of sharks will probably appear as, little by little, we and our miraculous technology turn our focus toward the sea. At least I hope we will, for our record so far has been nothing short of disgraceful.

We have seen less than 5 percent of our oceans; humans have actually visited less than 5 percent of that 5 percent.

We have studied the ocean so little compared to the earth that it's as if we dragged a butterfly net behind an airplane over the Grand Canyon at night and, based on what we collected, developed theories and generalizations about life on earth.

Here are some facts: nearly three-quarters of our home planet is covered by seawater (of an average depth of two miles); there are mountain ranges in the ocean higher than the Himalayas; there is enough gold suspended in seawater to supply every man, woman, and child on earth with a pound of the stuff; we can't even calculate how valuable the mineral, nutritional, and medicinal resources available in the sea might be. And yet for the past half century we have devoted much of our national treasure to reaching and studying a moon that we know to be barren, while spending, relatively, pennies on exploring our own oceans. More than forty years ago President John F. Kennedy was already lamenting that we knew more, even then, about the far side of the moon than we did about the bottom of the sea.

We know almost nothing about the ocean, so it's not surprising that we know so little about sharks.

Until recently, there's been no encouragement to learn about sharks, for sharks have never been popular. Whales, on the other hand, are enormously popular. The save-the-whales movement is more than thirty years old. And dolphins, of course, have long had large groups of devoted advocates.

It's true that whales and dolphins are easy to study and easier still to love. They're mammals. They breathe air. They nurse their young and guard them ferociously. They click and talk to one another. They do tricks. They're smart. We can project human characteristics onto them. We give them names and convince ourselves that they respond to—and even love—people they come to know.

Not sharks. Sharks are hard to study and harder still to love. Because they're fish, not mammals, they don't have to come up for air, so they're difficult to keep track of and impossible to count.

And they do have the unfortunate reputation of occasionally—very, very occasionally—attacking a human being. And—even more rarely—of eating one.

It's hard to care deeply for something that might turn on you and eat you.

Traditionally, shark scientists have been highly educated in the library and the laboratory and underexperienced in the field. But there have been—and are still—a handful of outstanding, dedicated shark scientists. They are rich in talent and widely experienced in the field.

Jaws brought me a lot of benefits, but the one I value most is the chance to do television shows and magazine stories with, and learn from, the scientists, sailors, fishermen, and divers who make the sea their home. The knowledge we've gained since the mid-1970s has convinced me that almost all of the great white shark behaviors I described in *Jaws* do happen in real life. But I'm also convinced that almost none of them happen for the reasons I described.

For example, what I and many others thought were attacks by great whites on boats were really explorations and samplings. In 1999, in the waters off Gansbaai, South Africa, I witnessed great-white behavior that would have been unimaginable even a few years before. Large adult great whites approached our tiny outboard-motor boats and permitted a "shark wrangler" named Andre Hartman to cup his hand over their snouts—a risky business. They rose out of the water, gaped for several seconds as if hypnotized, then slipped backward, down and away, in what looked like a swoon.

I am now convinced that attacks on human beings,

which I had thought were intentional, were mostly cases of mistaken identity. Sharks had been condemned as man-eaters for thousands of years, and it would be several more years before that belief would be effectively challenged.

We knew so little back then and have learned so much since, I couldn't possibly write the same story today. I know now that the mythic monster I created was largely a fiction.

I also know now, however, that the genuine animal is just as—if not even more—fascinating.

Most shark behaviors, it turns out, are explainable in logical, natural terms.

Sharks are critically important to the health of the oceans and the balance of nature in the sea. Later I'll go into detail about why I believe we should appreciate, respect, and protect sharks, rather than fear them.

First, though, let's take a look at some of the most dangerous sharks—the ones that have been called man-eaters.

7

Six Dangerous Sharks

There are, I believe, half a dozen species of sharks that can, and sometimes do, pose a threat to human beings.

THE GREAT WHITE

First and most notorious is the great white, the shark portrayed in *Jaws*. Great whites are the largest carnivorous fish in the sea. They can grow to be more than eighteen feet long and can weigh more than four thousand pounds. They can, and sometimes do, eat people, though it's now accepted that nearly every attack on a person is a mistake. The shark might confuse the person with a seal or sea lion. Or, particularly in murky water, where it must rely on senses other than vision, the shark takes a test bite to decide if this living thing is edible. There have been cases of great whites targeting humans. Few though they are, each case generates real horror.

A few years ago a woman who had been scuba diving near a seal colony was attacked in the waters off Tasmania.

She had almost gotten to the boat and was reaching out to grab her husband's hand when an enormous great white attacked her from behind and below. While her shocked husband held her hand, the shark bit her in half. Then it returned and took the upper half, literally yanking her torso from her husband's grasp.

Another notorious episode—and one for which no shark expert, scientist, or diver I've spoken with has ever offered a good explanation—occurred back in 1909. A fifteen-foot-long female great white was caught in the waters off the town of Augusta, Sicily. In her belly they found the remains of three human beings: two adults and a child.

More than 70 percent of victims of great-white shark attacks survive because the shark realizes it has made a mistake and doesn't finish off the prey. Granted, that figure doesn't take into account swimmers, divers, and snorkelers who simply disappear while swimming in great-white country.

The high rate of survival may have to do with something known as the "bite, spit, and wait" theory of great-white behavior. This theory was first advanced by Dr. John Mc-Cosker, senior scientist at the California Academy of Sciences. It explains both fatal attacks and attacks that end after a single bite. According to McCosker, great whites can tell in the microsecond of a first bite whether their potential prey has enough calories to be worth the effort. That is, if the prey won't deliver as much energy as the shark will use up in attacking and eating it, the shark breaks off the attack after a single bite. Depending on how serious that first bite is, the prey may or may not live to tell about it.

But if the first bite tells the shark that the prey contains a lot of energy—if it's a nice fat seal, for example, or a sea lion—it will hang around after the first bite. Then it will wait for its prey to bleed to death before it comes back to finish the meal.

In general, large great whites perceive human beings as too bony to bother with. So they often leave after that first bite. Of course, when a 2,000- or 3,000-pound fish tastes a 170-pound man, even one bite can be fatal. I will never forget a coroner's photographs of a young man killed in the Neptune Islands off South Australia. The shark must barely have grazed him before recognizing its mistake. Aside from one deep cut in a thigh and a nasty wound on one hand and wrist, the victim was unharmed. In the photographs he looked as if he was asleep. Sadly, however, the big shark's big teeth had opened two arteries, and the man had bled to death before he could reach the shore.

Some white-shark victims insist that they felt no pain at all when they were attacked, only the impact as they were struck. Then they felt a tug as the shark's scalpel-sharp teeth severed flesh and bone. My wife and I have a friend who lost a leg to a white shark while snorkeling off Australia. He said, "I couldn't see it, but I knew exactly what had me. It had me by the leg and was pulling me down. I thought for sure I was going to drown. I've never been so relieved in my life as when I felt my leg let go." Luckily for him, a boat was nearby. Someone aboard knew how to tie a tourniquet around his thigh, and he made it to a hospital.

From the swimmer's perspective, the best thing about great whites is that although they exist worldwide, they're extremely rare. Great whites are an apex predator, meaning they are at the top of the food chain. They are too powerful and devastating to exist in vast numbers: the marine food chain couldn't support them. So great whites breed late in life—not until they're at least twenty years old. And they bear very few young, only some of which survive to adulthood.

TIGER SHARKS

Tiger sharks, too, are genuinely dangerous to humans. They've been responsible for several attacks off Hawaii in recent years. On October 31, 2003, thirteen-year-old Bethany Hamilton, a top amateur surfer, was surfing with her best friend off the island of Kauai when a tiger shark bit off her left arm just below the shoulder. Her friend's father used a surf leash as a tourniquet to stop the bleeding; then fellow surfers put her on another surfboard and paddled her to shore. Their quick actions no doubt saved Bethany's life.

It's widely believed, with good reason, that tiger sharks pose more of a threat to humans than do great whites. Tigers may not be as big or as heavy as great whites, but a fifteen-foot, fifteen-hundred-pound tiger shark is plenty big enough. There are more of them, for they bear many more young than great whites (though sometimes the greedy young quickly eat each other). And they're everywhere. While great whites, as a rule, hang around coastal waters, tiger sharks are completely free-roaming. They're fond of coastal waters, and they like to enter lagoons at night and hunt in the shallows for prey that often includes smaller sharks. They also roam the deep.

Once, when I was on a boat over the abyssal canyons off Bermuda, a huge tiger shark cruised leisurely around our stern, as if showing off its amazing size. The top of its head was as big around as a manhole cover. The long, slender striped body seemed to take forever to pass by the stern. It was a chilling sight that reminded me of the crocodile in Peter Pan that waits for Captain Hook to fall overboard. To me, the message from this giant was *Take your time; no rush. I'm in no hurry. But sometime, someday, one of you will make a mistake and enter my realm, and then you'll be mine.*

Suddenly, though, the shark must have sensed that real potential prey was nearby. It sped away and a few seconds later exploded through the surface fifteen or twenty feet behind the boat. Clutched in its jaws was an adult sea turtle. The turtle was too big to swallow, and its shell was too tough to crack. It had pulled its head and legs into the safety of its shell. The shark shook the turtle violently from side to side.

Then, mysteriously, it let the turtle go and slipped silently beneath the surface.

For several moments we watched the turtle bobbing on the surface, head and legs still invisible. We guessed that the shark had given up and gone in search of easier prey. The turtle must have decided the same thing, for slowly its legs protruded from the shell, then came the head, and then . . .

Bammo! Like a rocket the shark blasted up from below. It clamped its jaws on one of the turtle's hind legs and didn't let go until the leg came off. The remaining three legs and the head snapped back inside the shell. Again the shark slid away underwater; again the turtle bobbed on the surface.

For the next half hour or so, we saw the attack repeated again and again, though without any more success. Once wounded, the turtle seemed ready to hunker down inside its shell forever, if necessary. As much as we rooted for the turtle—we knew it could live a successful life with three functioning legs—there was no way we could interfere. Nor did we want to, for this was normal, natural predation in the sea.

BULL SHARKS

The third shark that poses a true threat to humans in the sea is the bull shark. Bull sharks come in several varieties, including the Zambezi shark, the Lake Nicaragua shark, and several of the so-called whalers of Australia. As the first two names imply, bull sharks are even more wide-ranging than tigers. They have been found in—and have killed people in—lakes and rivers. Most sharks can't survive, not to mention hunt and feed, in brackish water. But bull sharks can function normally in salt, brackish, and fresh water.

Bull sharks are common in shallow water and murky water, like that off the Gulf Coast of Florida. It was a bull shark that attacked young Jesse Arbogast in July 2001, triggering the media frenzy that lasted all summer. And bull sharks were probably the culprits in the two nonfatal attacks a month later in the shallow waters off Grand Bahama Island. Bull sharks have such a bad reputation for being aggressive, fearless, and territorial that they undoubtedly are blamed for more attacks than they're responsible for. Still, there are so many bull sharks in so many waters in which so many people choose to swim that they must be classified as extremely dangerous.

OCEANIC WHITETIPS

Then there's the oceanic whitetip. Its Latin name describes the creature so perfectly that I'll burden you with it: *Carcharhinus longimanus,* or "long-hands." This shark's pectoral fins are extraordinarily long and graceful. They look like the wings of a modern fighter jet. *Longimanus* tends to stay in the deep ocean. Nobody on earth has the vaguest notion about total numbers of long-hand attacks.

That's because the people they do attack are either adrift, alone, or survivors of shipwrecks, who don't much care what species of shark it is that's harassing them.

I do know, however, that *longimanus* is unpredictable, scary, and capable of killing a human. There's a story about one that attacked two U.S. Navy divers in the deep waters of the Tongue of the Ocean in the Bahamas. The shark took a big bite out of one of the divers. Then, as the diver's buddy tried to hold on to his friend, it dragged the diver into the abyss. Finally, at a depth of about three hundred feet—far beyond safe scuba depth—the buddy had to choose between letting go of his friend and dying himself. He watched as shark and body disappeared into the gloom.

Long-hands are one of the few species of shark that genuinely terrify me. A couple of decades ago one made an honest effort to eat me. I don't blame the shark for trying, because my situation fell well within the bounds of Stupid Things You Should Avoid at All Costs. But the near miss still scared me—and scarred me permanently.

I was with an ABC-TV crew, also in the Tongue of the Ocean, in open water more than a mile deep. We had tied our boat to a navy buoy. The buoy had become a popular spot to film because it had been in the water for so long that the sea had claimed it, transforming it into an artificial reef. Microscopic animals had taken shelter in the buoy and the chain and had been followed by tiny crustacea and other small critters. Then larger and larger creatures had come to feed.

Finally—in the magical way the sea has of generating life on all levels—the entire food chain had come to use buoy and chain as a feeding ground.

A school of yellowfin tuna was swarming around the buoy, attracted by something. In the brilliant sunlight of the summer day the colors were gorgeous. So we decided to take some footage for the film segment about the Bahamas that we were working on for *The American Sportsman*.

I, as the so-called talent, was sent into the water. Stan Waterman followed to film whatever happened. We had only expected to film the contrasting colors of the beautiful fish against the greenish blue sea, interrupted now and then by a black-rubber-suited human.

Back then I was still a pretty raw blue-water diver. Blue-water diving is diving in water with no bottom visible or reachable. I wasn't used to diving in water more than five thousand feet deep. Once in a while I was haunted by a vision of my body drifting down, down, down, from light blue to darker blue, to purple and violet and the unknown black.

So, naturally, whenever I had to dive in blue water, I carried a security blanket: a sawed-off broomstick about three feet long, attached to my wrist by a rawhide thong. Exactly what it was supposed to protect me from I'm not sure. But I thought if cameramen carried cameras they could use to ward off attackers, and assistants carried cameras and lights, why shouldn't I be allowed to carry a broomstick?

Thus armed, I jumped overboard and swam among the

yellowfin tuna—or, rather, they swam around me. I held on to the barnacle-covered buoy chain to keep from being swept away by the current. The school of tuna, which had scattered when I splashed into the water, re-formed and circled me. The shafts of sunlight piercing the surface glittered on their silver scales and yellow fins. It seemed to me that Stan must be gathering an entire library of beauty shots.

The water was very clear. I was sure visibility was more than a hundred feet, though it's hard to tell in blue water, for there's nothing visible against which to gauge distances.

At the very edge of my vision I saw a shark swimming by. I couldn't tell what kind it was, and I didn't much care, for it showed no interest in me or the tuna.

Meanwhile, far up on the bow of the boat, one of the crew—bored and tantalized by the sight of so many delicious meals swimming so close to the boat—rigged a fishing rod. He dropped a baited hook into the water and let it drift back into the school of tuna. He had not asked permission, nor had he told anyone what he was doing. After all, he was staying out of the way and minding his own business. When he hooked a fish, he would simply haul it aboard, and no one need be the wiser.

Stan gestured for me to move away from the buoy so that he could frame me and the fish cleanly against the blue background. I let go of the chain and kicked my way out into open water. Obligingly, the tuna followed.

Suddenly I was gone, jerked downward by an irresistible

force, with a searing pain in my lower leg, arms flung over my head, broomstick aimed at the surface. I could see Stan and the tuna receding above me. I looked around, panicked and confused, to see what had grabbed me. The shark? Had I been taken by the shark? I saw nothing.

I looked down. I was already in the dark blue; all that lay below was the violet and the black. *Wait . . . there, against the darkness . . . what could it possibly—*

A tuna, fleeing for the bottom, struggling, fighting . . . *fighting? Against WHAT?*

Then I saw the line, and the silvery leader. The fish was *hooked*! Somehow it had gotten . . . *No, impossible, no way it could have—*

A cloud billowed around my face, black as ink, thick as . . . blood. *My blood.*

I leaned backward and kicked forward, wanting to see my feet.

The steel leader was wrapped around my ankle. The wire had bitten deep, and a plume of black was rising from the wound. That was a sign that I was already down very, very deep, for blood doesn't look black till the twilight depths. (The sea consumes the visible spectrum of light, one color at a time, beginning a few feet underwater. Red disappears first, then orange, yellow, green, and so on. When you reach 150 or 200 feet, blood looks black.)

All I could guess was that as the fish had fled the surface, it must have passed between my legs, or circled around my feet, or *somehow* wrapped the leader around my leg. And all I knew was that, somehow, I'd better find a way to free my leg before I was taken so deep that I would never return.

I reached for my knife, to cut the line. But first I couldn't find the knife, and then I couldn't release it.

The tuna stopped diving and turned. That relieved the pressure against its mouth and must have convinced it that it was free, for it swam upward, toward me.

The line slackened, and I slid my foot and fin out through the widening coil.

Giddy with relief, I checked my depth and air gauges: 185 feet deep, 500 pounds of air. That was more than enough for a controlled ascent.

I started up, slowly, and now the black blood no longer billowed around me but trailed behind. The pain in my leg had waned, and my foot seemed to be working, which meant that no major tendon had been cut.

I passed a hundred feet, then ninety, eighty. . . . Things were lighter now, visibility had returned, and I could see the rays of the sun angling down from the shimmering surface. Everything would be okay, after all. There was noth—

The shark came straight for me, emerging quickly from the blue haze. Its fins formed a lopsided triangle because of the slight downward curve of the extraordinary pectorals.

Ten, maybe fifteen feet from me it veered away. It banked downward and passed through the trail of blood leaking from my ankle. Now it was sure that I was the source of the tasty scent it had picked up from far away. It rose again, leveled off before me, and began the final stage of the hunt.

It's hard to be sure of sizes underwater. The generally accepted rule is that animals look about a third again as large as they actually are. This shark looked ten or twelve feet long, which meant that, in fact, it was probably seven to nine feet long. But "in fact" didn't matter to me. All I cared about was that the closer this shark came, the bigger it looked, and it was very big.

It circled me twice, perhaps twenty feet away. Then it gradually began to close the distance between us. With each circle, it came closer, first by six inches, then by twelve, then fifteen.

I raised my broomstick and held it out like a sword, waving its blunt tip back and forth. I wanted the shark to know that I was a living being armed with the weapons and determination to defend myself.

Longimanus was not impressed. It circled closer, staying just beyond the reach of the broomstick. I could count the tiny black dots on its snout. Those dots are called the ampullae of Lorenzini, and they carry untold megabytes of information, chemical and electromagnetic, to the shark's brain.

The mouth hung open about an inch, enough to give me a glimpse of the teeth in the lower jaw.

I turned with the shark, trying to maintain some upward

movement. I watched the eye—always the eye—for movement of the nictitating membrane. That would be the signal that the threat display was ending and the attack itself beginning.

It quickened its pace, circling me faster than I could turn. So I began to kick backward as well as upward, to increase the distance between us.

I jabbed randomly with the broomstick, never touching flesh, never causing *longimanus* even to flinch.

I glanced upward and saw the bottom of the boat, a squat, gray-black shape perhaps fifty feet away, forty-five, forty. . . .

The shark appeared from behind me, a pectoral fin nearly touching my shoulder. The mouth opened, and the membrane flickered upward, covering most of the eye. The upper jaw dropped down and forward, and the head turned toward me.

I remember seeing the tail sweep once, propelling *longimanus* forward.

I remember bending backward to avoid the gaping mouth.

I remember the ghostly, yellowish white eyeball, and I remember stabbing at it with the broomstick.

I don't remember hitting, instead, the roof of the shark's mouth. But that's what must have happened, for the next thing I knew, the shark bit down on the broomstick. It shook its head back and forth to tear it loose. When that failed, it lunged with its powerful tail, intent on fleeing with its prize.

The broomstick, of course, was attached to my wrist. I was suddenly dragged through the water like a rag doll, flopping helplessly behind the (by now) frightened shark. It had taken a test bite from a strange, bleeding prey and now found itself dragging a great rubber thing through the water.

Breathing became difficult; I was running out of air.

I tried to peel the rawhide thong off my wrist, but the tension on it was too great and I couldn't budge it.

I was on my back now, upside down, my right arm over my head as *longimanus* towed me away from the safety of the boat. I could once again see blood trailing from my leg. At this depth it was dark blue, and it streamed behind me like a wake.

Everything stopped. At once. My arm was free, and I was floating about thirty feet beneath the surface. I looked at the broomstick—or at what remained of it. *Longimanus* had bitten through it.

Far away, at the outer limits of my sight, I saw the black scythe of a tail fin vanish into the blue.

I sucked one final breath from my tank, opened my mouth, and tipped my head back. I kicked a couple of times and rose up to the kingdom of light and air.

Not until I reached the swim step at the stern of the boat did the weakness of fear overcome me, and the shock.

I spat out my mouthpiece, took off my mask, and started cursing that so-and-so of a shark.

"No!" said the director. "No, no, no. You can't use that language on network television. Go back down and surface again and tell us what you saw."

MAKOS AND BLUE SHARKS

The final two sharks on my personal list of species to be wary of could not be more different from each other. One, the mako, is a loner that's sleek, silent, and vicious. The other, the blue shark, is a pack animal that rarely bothers anyone. But it has, on occasion, killed human beings floating in the ocean. Because it is a pelagic (open-water) shark like *longimanus,* the blue shark is vulnerable to large commercial fishing operations. Over the last ten years, populations of blues all over the world have been devastated.

The mako is one of the fastest fish in the sea—far and away the fastest shark. It is the only shark listed by the International Game Fishing Association as a true "sport fish." The feel of most sharks on a fishing line is like hauling on wet laundry or trying to lift a cow. Fighting a mako has been compared to riding a bull or wrestling an enraged crocodile.

Makos leap completely out of the water, turn somersaults, and "run" in any and all directions in their frenzy to escape. Hooked makos have been known to charge boats and jump into open cockpits, where they've gone berserk and destroyed the craft that has hooked them. (A mako can weigh more than a thousand pounds.) Some fishermen have jumped overboard rather than risk being beaten to death by the flailing fish. A few have tried to subdue maddened makos by shooting at them with high-powered rifles—a dangerous move, because of possible unintended consequences such as putting a hole in the boat, or in a companion.

While the body of a mako is one of the most beautiful in the sea, its face is positively ugly. A mako looks mean. Its teeth, upper and lower, are long, pointed, sharp as needles, and snaggly. A great white's teeth speak to me of quick, efficient death. But a mako's teeth warn of a nasty end, of flesh ripped into ragged chunks. A mako's eye, too, is distinct from every other shark's. To me, at least, it looks crazed and threatening, ready at any second to explode into unstoppable violence.

A mako's speed, however, is its most dazzling weapon. Especially over short distances—like the range of visibility in most water conditions—it can appear and disappear as if by magic. It's a gray ghost in the distance one second, right in front of you the next, gone the next, back again the next.

A friend of mine was snorkeling in shallow water in the Bahamas a few years ago. He was poking the sand bottom with a long metal rod in search of buried cannons or shipwreck wood. When he glanced up he noticed a shark cruising at the far limit of his vision. Here's what he recalls:

"I didn't give it a thought, didn't pay any mind to what kind it was. Before my eyes had refocused on the bottom, it hit me. Out of nowhere. I never saw it coming. All I knew was I felt like I'd been hit by a freight train. My mask was knocked off, both flippers came off, I dropped the spear, and suddenly the water was full of blood. Mine. The mako had hit me just once, a glancing blow, tore up my thigh pretty badly. I could see him off a ways, hanging there, like he was deciding whether or not I was worth eating. Then—poof!— he was gone. I guess he figured I was too bony."

Bony, perhaps; lucky, definitely.

ANY SHARK CAN RUIN YOUR DAY

Don't take as gospel my (or anybody's) list of bad actors in the company of sharks. All such lists are subjective. Mine includes only sharks that either I or my colleagues have had trouble with. Some folks, for instance, have reason to be scared of hammerheads. Others have had unhappy run-ins with gray reef sharks.

What you *should* take as gospel is that *any* shark *can* be dangerous. Still, most injuries inflicted by reputedly inoffensive sharks are caused by human error or ignorance.

Nurse sharks, for example, are among the gentlest of all shark species. The common peril people face from them is being bumped by them as they flee. I know of one diver, however, who entered a cave and saw a nurse shark sleeping in the sand. He pulled the shark's tail to get it to move. The shark moved, all right. Startled awake, it spun around in a frantic blur and bit the man in the throat (missing an artery by a couple of millimeters). It tore a gold chain from his neck, and as it fled the cave, it knocked the man spinning against the rock wall.

Over a single August weekend in 2001, in the single Florida county of Volusia, six people were bitten by sharks *that they had seen before they entered the water*. The sharks (most were blacktips) had gathered to feed on schools of baitfish. The people had gathered for a surfing contest. Too impatient to wait for the sharks to finish feeding and leave the area, the surfers chose instead to wade among and step over the feeding sharks.

That only six were bitten seems to me a miracle.

Other attacks have happened to people who ignored, or were ignorant of, the basic rules that help keep the chances of an attack to a minimum. They swam at dawn or at dusk; they swam alone; they swam far from shore or where fish were feeding or birds were working.

On August 19, 2003, Debra Franzman, age fifty, was swimming with seals at Avila Beach, California, when she was fatally bitten by a great white shark. She was wearing a black wet suit with a black hood, booties, and gloves. To the shark she undoubtedly looked like a wounded (or extremely clumsy) seal floundering around on the surface. As risky as such behavior sounds—and is—she had apparently been swimming with those same seals and wearing that same costume nearly every day for ten years—completely without incident.

Elsewhere in the world, a man was almost killed when he tried to hitch a ride on the back of a whale shark, as harmless a giant as ever roamed the sea. When he grabbed the enormous dorsal fin, his hand slipped; then he slipped. He hung in the water, watching, as the great speckled body moved beneath him like a ship. He forgot that this ship was driven not by a propeller but by a tail as tall as he was and as hard as iron. The sweeping tail clubbed him from behind, leaving him breathless and senseless. He survived only because an alert buddy located his regulator mouthpiece, rammed it into his mouth, and purged it—forcing air into him. Then the buddy inflated his vest, which lifted him to the surface.

There is one circumstance under which any shark of any size will eat a human being without hesitation. That is if the person is dead.

Sharks are scavengers. Scouring and clearing the ocean of animals that are weak, weary, or dead is one of a shark's most valuable functions.

8
Swimming Safely in the Sea

At approximately nine o'clock on the morning of July 23, 2001, four young cousins—three girls and a boy, aged eleven to sixteen—waded into knee-deep water at a beach in Far Rockaway, Queens, New York. The lifeguards assigned to the beach were not scheduled to begin their shift for another hour. But the cousins were with an adult, an uncle, who was aware of the dangerous currents off this particular stretch of beach. He warned his nieces and nephew not to go into the water, while he prepared fishing rods and fetched food for their picnic.

The girls and boy probably thought they were obeying; wading wasn't really going into the water.

Within minutes, three of them were dead.

While the uncle's attention was elsewhere, all four had been yanked off their feet by the waves. They were grabbed and dragged underwater by a current so violent that it had already earned the area its local nickname—"the death trap." Only one of the kids, the eleven-year-old boy, managed somehow to escape the grip of the current and get back to shore.

The next day's newspapers were full of warnings against swimming on unguarded beaches. Officials warned about the price the public pays for ignoring regulations.

But the real reason those three girls drowned and about 3,500 other people in the United States drown every year has nothing to do with rules, regulations, or lifeguards.

It has to do with the public's unfamiliarity with the ocean and its ignorance about swimming safely in it.

According to the American Red Cross, more than 54 percent of Americans—perhaps as many as 140 million people—say that their primary leisure activity is swimming. That's more than all our golfers, tennis players, sailors, scuba divers, and Frisbee players combined. Off the record, though, those same Red Cross officials say that only about 12 percent of those swimmers are actually competent in the water.

And who knows what tiny fraction of that 12 percent are competent ocean swimmers. That's a specialty that takes as much knowledge, training, and experience as rock climbing or kayaking. A Red Cross–certified beginning swimmer is about as close to a skilled ocean swimmer as a licensed driver is to an Indianapolis 500 contestant.

The United States has 12,383 miles of shoreline. Much less than 1 percent is patrolled by lifeguards on any given day. So if, on a hot summer day, you're struck by a sudden urge to swim in the sea, the odds are that there won't be a lifeguard nearby to keep an eye on you.

I began to swim in the ocean at the age of five. I went with an uncle who had been disqualified from serving in the armed forces during World War II because of a bad back. Swimming in the sea was his passion and his therapy. Because there were no lifeguards on most of the beaches on Nantucket, he wanted me to know how to take care of myself.

He taught me how to study the water before I went in and how to enter the water without getting bashed by a wave. He taught me how to select a good wave to ride, how to ride it, and how to recover from the mistakes I was bound to make. He taught me that swimming in the ocean meant working with the ocean, never against it.

My uncle's first lesson was: *Never fight the ocean. Go with it and it will work with you. Let it take you where it will, and it will let you go.*

It's the most important single thing to know about ocean swimming. If everyone who swam in the ocean obeyed it, the number of drownings would shrink dramatically.

People who get into trouble in the ocean tend to panic. Somewhere between twenty and forty people *a day* will drown during the summer in the United States. Most of them will be within fifteen feet of safety, but they will drown because they panic.

If you are a young, healthy person, there is no reason for you to drown while swimming in the ocean. But before you enter the water, you need to learn the basic facts about the environment into which you're about to go. Some people believe that they can outmuscle the ocean. No one can. And yet there are some who will die trying.

Here are some basic lessons I've learned and some simple precautions that will help keep you from getting into trouble while swimming off a beach. You just need to learn a little about how oceans work, have the patience to study the water you're about to enter, and use your common sense.

NEVER SWIM ALONE

Never, never, never, under any circumstances. There are too many things that can go wrong—from getting cramps to choking on salt water to being stung by jellyfish or micro-scopic organisms—for anyone to risk swimming without assistance nearby. Lifeguards aren't enough; they can take too long to reach you, especially if you're choking or gagging.

OCEAN WATER IS ALWAYS MOVING

This is a fact you must take on faith. No matter how calm the surface may appear, the water beneath is never still.

It is moving in three directions: back and forth along the shore, in and out from the beach, and up and down along the slope of the shelf of the beach.

Water is driven constantly by wind, tides, and currents, and by local factors like channels, jetties, and points of land. The presence (or absence) of reefs, shoals, and sandbars will change water's motion. Prevailing winds will drive surf onto certain beaches and leave others to be lapped by little but the tides.

If you intend to swim in the ocean, it makes sense to stand for a moment and study what the water is doing that day. The wind will be pushing waves onto the beach. Since winds rarely blow directly at a beach, the waves will strike the shore at an angle. This causes a current called a set or a drift that moves the water in a particular direction.

Look at swimmers already in the water or at pieces of wood or seaweed floating on the surface. Note which way they're moving and how fast. That will tell you how strong the drift is and how quickly you'll be carried away from the point where you enter the water. The stronger the drift, the closer you should stay to shore. If the drift is strong, carefully plan where you want to exit the water, because here is another fact of ocean swimming: *You Cannot Swim Against a Strong Current.* If you try, you will exhaust yourself. You could start a chain of events that may lead to disaster: fatigue, gasping, breathing water, choking, panic, struggling for air, waving or calling for help, sinking, and, finally, drowning.

If you want to come out of the water near your blanket, your soda, and your can of Pringles, walk up the beach in the opposite direction of the drift. Enter the water, and let yourself float down the beach until you reach your exit point. Then swim gently across the drift toward shore. Otherwise, be prepared to float away from your home base and walk back when you're finished swimming. Under *no* circumstances should you try to swim against the current.

There are a few naturally occurring phenomena that can sometimes (but not always) be seen from the shore. They can be deadly but don't have to be. You can anticipate them just by being aware of them, whether or not you see them coming.

UNDERTOW

This is a term that is universally known and widely misunderstood. Many people use *undertow* to mean *any* action of waves, currents, or tides that can be dangerous. In fact, undertow occurs mostly on narrow beaches with steep drop-offs. It is, simply, the action of water thrown ashore by a wave returning to the sea.

After a wave breaks, gravity will carry the water back to sea. If the drop-off into the sea is steep, the water will fall sharply, carrying you with it. If you don't struggle or resist, the undertow will carry you for a few feet (perhaps more, but not much more) and will then fade away. Buoyed by the air in your lungs, you will rise to the surface, and you can swim back to shore. You may find yourself in water over your head. But if you're not comfortable being in water deeper than you are tall, you should probably not be swimming in the ocean in the first place.

RUNOUT OR SEA PUSS

A common cause of problems is known both as a runout and a sea puss. Somewhere offshore from a fairly straight beach there may be an invisible sandbar or shoal that has built up over a long period. Millions of tons of water will flow over the bar toward shore. At last, the level of the water inside the bar will be greater than the water level outside the bar. Then the water must begin to flow back seaward.

If there is a weak spot in the sandbar, it may collapse and create a funnel-like path through the bar. The enormous volume of water will rush toward the funnel with unimaginable power and irresistible force.

Runouts happen frequently, and they can be seen from the beach. People watching one have described the scene as like seeing the entire ocean running down a drain. A strip of water leading out to sea, perhaps ten yards wide, perhaps fifty, will look different from the rest of the ocean. It will definitely have its own motion. It may contain short, choppy, foamy waves. The water will look murky and sandy from turbulence. All kinds of flotsam—pieces of wood, seaweed, trash—will be speeding seaward in the strip. If there is wave action over the sandbar, the runout will look like a gap in the surf, for this is where the bar has collapsed. Once beyond the sandbar, the strip will vanish as the water disperses and the runout has . . . well . . . run out.

For veteran surfers, runouts are a blessing. They provide effortless transport over the bar and beyond the waves. Surfers know that if they change their minds, they can return to calm water simply by paddling across the runout until they're out of it.

Swimmers caught in runouts have that option, too. But most either don't know it or, in shock and surprise, forget it. They panic and try to resist the force of the runout. Instead, they should surrender to it and, when they're ready, swim across and out of it.

Swimmers caught in a runout have another option, too, but it takes a cool head and a practiced eye to choose it. If you can see the sandbar offshore (or the waves breaking on it) and can tell that it isn't too far to swim safely back from, you can—no kidding—relax and enjoy the ride. The runout will carry you past the bar. A little farther out it will fade away. Then you can return to shore—maybe even pleasantly, by riding one or more of the waves that break over the bar.

That second option may be a bit of a challenge for the average swimmer. But once more, if you're not fit enough to swim, kick, float, or dog-paddle for a couple of hundred yards in the ocean, don't go in.

Undertows and runouts affect only swimmers. They occur in the water or, in the case of runouts, offshore. You can't be caught in one if you don't go swimming. But there is one ocean menace that can reach up onto the beach and grab you and drag you into deep water. Its common name is a rip.

RIP

The reason a rip is so dangerous is that it actually forms on the beach. If you are wading in the wave wash where a rip begins—like the four kids in Queens mentioned earlier—you can be knocked off your feet and sucked out to sea in a matter of seconds.

Beaches are by nature unstable. The mixture of sand, pebbles, rocks, shells, vegetation, and water that makes up a beach is soft. Its shape changes with every wave that passes through and over it. All day long erosion creates small depressions up and down the beach. Water from returning waves will flow toward the depressions, scouring them deeper and wider and creating, very quickly, a strong seaward pull—a rip.

If you are standing at the edge of such a depression, the ground will suddenly disappear and you will be sucked away from shore. If the natural slope of the beach is long, gentle, and shallow, you may be able to struggle out of the rip, sideways, into calm water. But if the slope is short and steep, you will be in deep water before you can catch a breath.

Rips look like runouts, and you can get out of them safely in the same ways. Like a runout, a rip is a strip of rough, murky, foamy water moving directly away from the beach. A rip begins right at the beach, however, and it tends to be narrower than a runout, anywhere from a few feet to a few yards wide. It doesn't travel as far—usually it fades away just beyond the breakers. It can end as suddenly and unpredictably as it began, while other ones may be forming at other spots along the same beach.

A swimmer caught in a rip has the same options as a swimmer caught in a runout. You can swim across the rip until you're out of it, or let it carry you out until its force diminishes. Whatever you do, *don't fight it.* Don't try to swim straight back to the beach. That way lie exhaustion, panic, and, perhaps, drowning.

To me, one of the saddest things about drowning is that it is so often so easy to prevent.

Years ago, I wrote a piece for the *New York Times Magazine* on how to swim safely in the ocean. In it I quoted veteran Red Cross safety expert Mike Howes, who described for me the typical drowning victim:

"He [the victim] decides he's in trouble, so to attract

attention he waves his arms over his head, which puts a lot of meat out of water—where it's heavier—and makes him sink. He struggles up again, gasps for breath, then waves his arms again and sinks again. If he left his arms in the water and waved them slowly up and down, he'd stay on the surface. But he doesn't, so he gets water in his mouth; his epiglottis slams shut, and he panics. He coughs, sinks, coughs underwater, gasps, and—well, that's it."

What most swimmers don't know is that if they are un-injured and even a little competent, they can save them-selves. In all but the roughest and coldest seas, they can stay afloat indefinitely. They can also, without great effort, move toward shore. They may end up several miles from where they entered the water, but they'll be alive to gripe about the walk home.

One day in my late teens I was swimming with a friend off the south shore of Nantucket when we found ourselves trapped beyond the breaking point of endless, tremendous waves. There were no surfboards, body boards, or Boogie boards back then—at least not on Nantucket. All we had for flotation and transportation were our own air-filled lungs and our own strong arms and legs. We had been riding the waves happily for an hour or so and had paid no attention to where we were in relation to the shore. We weren't aware that we had been swept away from the long, sloping beach where the waves broke in regular rhythms and carried us all the way in to knee-deep water. Now, we were surprised to find, we were far offshore from a steep, relatively short beach. That beach combined with a hidden sandbar to produce row after row of tall, rough waves that crested high and broke almost straight downward.

We tried to ride waves. But instead of being carried gently ashore, we were slammed violently onto the hard-sand bottom, "boiled" mercilessly in the sandy foam, and then pushed upward to more or less the same place where we had begun. All this just in time to duck under another monster wave, and another. After making almost no progress for ten or fifteen minutes, we were both exhausted. We knew that our only hope lay farther offshore, in the calm water beyond the waves.

Turning seaward, we swam under breaking wave after breaking wave. Finally, we reached open water where ocean swells had not yet become waves.

We were, we guessed, between a quarter and half a mile offshore. Though we couldn't see the waves actually breaking onshore, we could see their massive shoulders gather and hunch before they disappeared. They were instantly followed by the next rank of waves and the next.

We knew very well that there was no way we were going to make it to shore in these conditions. We also knew, though, that we really had nothing to worry about. Nantucket is only fourteen miles long. We had entered the water at about the midpoint of the island, and we were heading westward. There, at the end of the island, shallow shoals extended far offshore.

We were cold, yes, because the water temperature was only in the upper seventies. But if we stayed active, we could keep from freezing for many hours. We might run into a serious stroke of bad luck—getting eaten by something, say, or getting run down by a nuclear submarine. But the odds against either of those things happening were astronomical. We knew we could float safely until we reached a time of slack tide or a point at which we could walk ashore.

We'd be inconvenienced, surely, and grumpy and tired and cold. We'd be forced to catch a ride, soaking wet and sandy, back to our car. But we would be alive.

It took four hours, but that's what happened. Along the way, we passed several populated beaches. The people were so far away that they looked like the tiny computer-generated passengers in the movie *Titanic*. We even passed a beach with a lifeguard, but we raised no alarm. We didn't want to put anyone's life in jeopardy by asking them to rescue us. Besides, we were fine; we didn't need rescue.

Sometime in the afternoon, we came to a part of the island where the shoals extended so far out to sea that wave action stopped. There was no steep beach for the waves to break on. We were in a stretch of choppy sea that we could, at first, swim through and then, at last, wade through.

We were as grumpy and tired and cold as I had predicted—and we were grateful. I said a silent thank-you to my uncle.

DROWNPROOFING: A SURVIVAL TECHNIQUE

Everyone who wants to swim in the sea should learn an excellent survival technique called drownproofing. It was invented in the 1940s by a swimming coach named Fred Lanoue. Endorsed by the U.S. Public Health Service and taught at many schools, it's easy to learn and, as much as anything can be, idiotproof. (It is not, however, panicproof. Nothing is.)

The two ideas behind drownproofing are: (1) most people will float if their lungs are filled with air; and (2) it's much easier and less tiring to float vertically than horizontally. Most people's bodies *want* to float vertically, buoyed by the two big air sacs (the lungs) that stay near the surface, and with the heavy (bony and muscular) hips and legs dangling beneath.

Here's how to drownproof yourself with an adult's supervision:

Floating vertically, with your hands limp at your sides, take a deep breath. Hold it, and let yourself hang there, with your face in the water and your eyes closed.

As soon as you feel that you'd like to take a breath—

long before that awful feeling when you know you *must*—exhale slowly through your nose. Raise your arms, and cross them in front of your face. Spread them as if you were parting curtains. When your arms are extended, push your palms down toward your sides and tilt your head back. Your mouth will come out of the water. Take a breath, lower your head and arms, and let yourself bob in the water.

Every movement should be easy, deliberate, unhurried. You're not trying to go anywhere. There's no rush and no worry. When you hear your pulse—and you will, for the rhythms of your body become the focus of your mind—it should sound normal, not rapid. Fear and excitement waste energy and oxygen.

I can hear you muttering, "Easy for *you* to say." But that's why you're practicing, so that if the time comes for you to save yourself, you'll be ready.

It won't take you long to feel at ease with the technique of drownproofing. When you do, lift your head out of the water and flutter-kick gently until your body is horizontal. Then—on your back, with your hands paddling easily at your sides—kick as often as is comfortable in the general direction of the shore.

If you tire, stop kicking. Let your legs hang down again, and resume the drownproofing breathing until you feel you're ready to carry on. Remind yourself that you're not trying to "beat" the sea, nor is it trying to beat you.

We humans sometimes tend to assign human characteristics not only to animals but to the sea itself. We use words like *treacherous, savage,* and *killer* to describe natural phenomena like waves, currents, and storms. We refuse to accept that we must coexist with nature, not compete with it or attempt to dominate it.

We are nature, and nature is us. We are of the sea and from the sea. If we choose to go into the sea, we must respect and appreciate it. It is an environment that is different but not hostile to the educated and prepared, and fatal mostly to the foolhardy.

9
How to Avoid a Shark Attack

Remember: the chances of your being killed by a shark are so tiny, they're not worth worrying about.

The odds against being *attacked* by a shark are nearly as long. Very, very few encounters between swimmers or snorkelers and sharks result in what could be considered an actual *attack*.

I think of an attack as what a grizzly bear does when she's protecting her cubs, or what wolves, bears, and even rats do when they're cornered or threatened. In general, sharks do not attack people. The exceptions happen mostly to scuba divers who cross an invisible line into an area that a shark considers its territory. Then the divers don't see, don't understand, or choose to ignore the obvious warnings issued by the shark.

When a shark feels threatened or crowded, its posture changes. Its back hunches; its pectoral fins drop; sometimes it shakes its head back and forth; always it looks and acts agitated. It is saying—*shouting*—"Get out of here! This is my turf." Fish get the message; they scatter and disappear into the reef. People sometimes don't. Then the shark attacks: it rushes in, bites, and, usually, retreats to wait and see if the intruder leaves.

For the most part, what we're talking about when we use the words *shark attack* are really shark *bites*. They are a part of the shark's normal feeding pattern, motivated not by rage, fear, or frenzy but by curiosity, confusion, and hunger.

I'll repeat, the chances of your being bitten by a shark are ridiculously small. But if you swim in the sea, the possibility does exist. The good news is that there are ways to reduce the odds to very close to zero.

Over the past twenty-five years, in the United States and many other countries around the world, there has been a vast shift in population toward the seashore. In the United States alone, some 50 percent of our 280 million people now live within 50 miles of the shore. Millions of people who did not grow up near the sea and who know nothing about it are now exposing themselves to the sea, with all its beauty, power, mystery, and danger.

Many people who swim in the sea do not give it respect for what it is: the largest environment on the planet, home to more animals than any other. All of those animals must eat in order to survive. It is an environment in which most of us are aliens—clumsy aliens who are ill equipped to survive.

And yet on every glorious day of every summer, boys, girls, and adults around the world plunge into the sea.

They take risks that they shouldn't, most involving drowning but some involving creatures that sting, pinch, and bite—including sharks.

That's why I believe that practically no shark bite is unprovoked. We provoke sharks simply by going into the water, entering their feeding grounds, becoming fair game.

There are some practical guidelines to follow to reduce the risk of a shark bite. The first requires a bit of a change in the way we look at the world.

These days, most of us are rarely in danger from anything in nature. As a result, we've come to assume we're safe everywhere. We tend to see every animal as warm, cuddly, and friendly, or sometimes simply afraid of us. So little are we exposed to wild animals that we have no real knowledge of how to behave around them.

On land, our ignorance is rarely tested. Deer eating flowers in the backyard aren't a threat to life and limb. But when we choose to go into the sea, we can't afford to make mistakes. Many millions of creatures live in the sea. Among them is a large, free-roaming predator that poses a real threat to humans: the shark.

And sharks can be anywhere: in shallow water or deep, even in the surf itself. They can be in the little dips between the shore and sandbars just offshore, where low tide sometimes traps them. They can be in murky water or clear, rough water or calm.

While only a few species of sharks are considered dangerous to humans, *all* sharks—especially those more than three feet long—should be respected and avoided by swimmers. I've been hassled by a school of three- and four-foot-long sharks. What began as a game of push-and-shove soon turned into a terrifying mass mugging from which I barely escaped, with bite marks on my fins.

Before you enter the water, stand for a moment and look at the sea around you. Are there birds working offshore—swooping and diving into a school of baitfish near the surface? That's a sign that larger predators are underneath, driving the baitfish upward.

Perhaps those predators are bass or bluefish. But a shark or two could be stalking the bass or bluefish. Any signs that schools of fish are in the neighborhood might mean that sharks are there, too. If you see a concentration of ripples on the surface of the water, or silvery flashes as feeding fish roll out of the water and their scales catch the sunlight, or a patch of action anywhere in an otherwise calm sea, don't go into the water. Nature's food chain is in progress. There's always a chance that the apex predator is out hunting, too.

Don't go into the water if you're bleeding—at all, from anything, anywhere on your body. The same salt water that may heal your cut will carry away the scent of your blood. The senses of sharks are so finely tuned that they can receive and analyze the tiniest bits of blood imaginable. And the shark can home in on the source of the blood from far, far away.

Blood is not the only thing that attracts sharks to us humans. We emit sounds, smells, pressure waves, and electromagnetic fields—all of which a shark can detect. That shouldn't surprise you. A dog or cat hears and sees in spectral ranges far beyond ours, so why shouldn't a shark? After all, sharks have been around, and have been very successful, for scores of millions of years longer than cats, dogs, and people.

Don't swim or surf in water near seal or sea lion colonies. These playful mammals are the prime (and favorite) food source for great white sharks, among others. When seen from below, a surfer on a board looks just like a sea lion that has gone up for a breath of air. Great whites are, by nature, ambushers—they prefer to blindside their prey. They attack from below and behind, and with such speed and force that they sometimes bite through surfboard *and* surfer before they realize they've made a mistake.

Don't go swimming at dawn, dusk, or night. Many sharks—tigers, for example—come into the shallows at night to feed. On some islands, locals swear that sharks can tell when six o'clock in the evening comes along. That's when fins can be seen crisscrossing the bay or cruising along the beach. Dim light also makes it harder for a shark to see. Then it must rely on its other senses, which increases the chances of a random bite.

The same holds true for swimming in murky water. A shark may sense nearby movement of a warm-blooded animal it can't see. It may decide to take a bite to determine if the animal is tasty.

Don't swim alone, and don't swim far from shore or other people. As a lone swimmer you are vulnerable prey—and the farther you are from rescue if something does go wrong, the lower your chances of survival.

Don't go swimming where people are fishing from boats. They've probably put bait in the water, or even chum, which is a mixture of blood, oil, guts, and fish bits. (Even if you're not set upon by a shark, you'll stink for days, especially your hair.)

Finally, and most obviously, don't go swimming in areas where sharks gather or feed. These include steep drop-offs, where tide and current sweep prey to waiting sharks, and the passes in tropical lagoons, where every six hours, the change of tide brings new feeding patterns to the entire chain of wildlife in the water. Avoid channels into harbors, where fish are cleaned and their remains tossed overboard from returning boats.

There are also a few don'ts for when you *do* go swimming.

Don't wear jewelry or any shiny metal in the water. It flashes and shines and can, in murky water, look to a shark like a wounded fish. A friend of mine went swimming wearing a bathing suit with a brass buckle. As he was wading out of chest-deep water, he felt something brush between his legs. When he reached the beach he found that he'd been slashed open from thigh to knee—by something with extremely sharp teeth, either a barracuda or a small shark, for he never felt any pain. If there hadn't been a lifeguard handy to put a tourniquet around his leg, he might have bled to death.

Another friend wore a gold cross on a gold chain while he was snorkeling. A shark rushed him from below, ripped cross and chain away, and, with the same slashing bite, tore open his chin.

Don't swim in the ocean with your dog. Dogs swim with a jerky, ungainly motion that can attract curious sharks.

And don't you make any jerky movements, either, such as splashing, kicking, or tussling with your buddy. All of those send out signals that say *Wounded prey . . . worth investigating.*

Despite all these cautions, it's important to remember that no matter what you do, the odds are in your favor. Whether or not a person acts carefully and with common sense, the chances of being attacked by a shark remain somewhere between slim and none.

10

When Good Dives Go Bad

Usually when you're diving, you don't want to see sharks any more than you want to meet up with a bear while you're walking in the woods or with a pack of wolves while you're cross-country skiing.

Apex predators are the creatures at the top of the food chain that generally have no natural enemies except others of their own species (and, of course, humans). They have a way of spoiling your whole day, even if they don't chase you down and tear you to bits in a bizarre fit of madness or hunger.

If you've had good training or a lot of experience as a diver, you know how to cope with common emergencies. No matter how experienced or well trained you are, however, you can never be completely prepared for the sudden appearance of one or more aggressive sharks. The reason? Here it comes again: *No matter how much we think we know, the truth is, none of us knows for certain what any shark will do in a given situation.*

The tiger sharks I dove with in Australia were interested in nothing but the bait laid out for them. Luckily for me, they dismissed humans—*these* humans, at least—as of no interest.

In the Sea of Cortez I dove with vast schools of scalloped hammerheads. There were so many that seen from beneath, they blocked out the sun. Not once did one of them express anything more than idle curiosity about us.

In deep water off Rangiroa, an atoll in the Tuamotu chain of islands in French Polynesia, photographer David Doubilet and I pursued five enormous great hammerheads. Great hammerheads are a species unto themselves, very different from the schooling scalloped hammerheads. These five were hefty, robust females, all fifteen feet or longer. Any one of them could have consumed either of us in two bites. But not one would pause long enough for David to take a photograph.

Rangiroa is also home to a small but healthy population of silky sharks. Silkies are a particularly "sharky"-looking type of shark, with a supersleek body and a perfect shark profile. They are considered dangerous to humans, but I've dived with the ones around Rangiroa half a dozen times or more, and I've never had trouble with any of them. Once there was a misunderstanding of signals between David and me. He was signaling that he was ill and about to vomit into his regulator. But I thought he was signaling me to get closer to the shark. So I let a large silky come so close to my head that I could count the pores on its snout and see the texture of its yellowish eyeball. When at last I realized what was happening, I shrugged one of my shoulders, nudging the silky in the jaw, and it sped away.

Nor have I had trouble with any of the various kinds of bull sharks. But I know that many people—divers as well as swimmers—have. If I see a bull shark underwater, I never take my eyes off it. I am convinced that bull sharks are dangerous to human beings, and they deserve a bigger dose of fear than most other species.

I'm just as wary of makos, though they're so fast that keeping them in sight is nearly impossible. Not only are makos the fastest sharks in the sea, and armed with a mouthful of scraggly knives, but they also have a reputation for crankiness.

I've been in the water with a mako only once. It appeared as if by magic and paused no more than two feet in front of cinematographer Stan Waterman. Before Stan could focus his camera, his safety diver—whose sole job is to watch the cameraman's back—panicked. He whacked the mako with his "bang stick," a steel tube fitted on one end with a twelve-gauge-shotgun blank and a detonating mechanism. The explosion of the gases inside the cartridge blew a hole the size of a silver dollar in the mako's head, killing it instantly. We watched the beautiful metallic blue body swirl away into the darkness of the deep.

Stan was furious. He had detected no danger, he had had

the mako in sight at all times, and it hadn't threatened him once. The gorgeous animal had died for nothing. Stan's safety diver was embarrassed and apologetic.

And then, finally, there is the shark for which no amount of instruction, training, warning, or anticipation can prepare a diver: the great white. Yes, there are a few helpful things to know. For example, you can reduce the creature's advantage by letting it know that *you* know it sees you. Great whites are ambushers, preferring to attack prey from below and behind. Theoretically, if you face down a great white, you may convince it that you're too much trouble to bother with. Theoretically.

I know someone in South Africa who snorkels and scuba dives with great whites in the open (that is, with no cage). He sometimes carries for protection a weighted piece of wood painted to look like an enormous great white's head in "full gape"—mouth yawning open, upper jaw down and out in bite position. He claims that his bluff has several times deceived great whites and discouraged them from attacking him.

Still, nothing in the world can prepare the average scuba diver for an unplanned encounter with whitey. I know it to be true, for it happened to me several years ago.

I was on a trip with Teddy Tucker, a man with a vast knowledge of the sea. Teddy was asked to journey to Walker's Cay in the Bahamas, to study a pile of ancient cannons that had been discovered on the sandy bottom. The finder of the cannons wanted Teddy's opinion as to whether the guns were signs of a shipwreck in the immediate vicinity. If they were, he might finance an archaeological expedition to preserve the ship's remains. On the other hand, the cannons might only be a "dump." That is, they might have been tossed overboard centuries before from a storm-wracked ship trying to lighten itself enough to pass over the reefs and shoals where it was trapped. Teddy would scour the rocks and coral nearby for river stones that might have been used as ballast. He would search for bits of wood or metal and for corals that could signal iron, bronze, silver, or sections of a ship's skeleton concealed beneath.

I went with Teddy not because he needed me but because I knew that a trip with Teddy was an adventure guaranteed. His trips were always fascinating, often exciting, and sometimes dangerous. I had already written two novels inspired by escapades with Teddy, *The Deep* and *The Island,* and more were to follow.

It took him only a few dives over a couple of days to conclude that the cannons were a dump. No ship had sunk with them—no ship big enough to carry so many guns, anyway, and none right there. Perhaps the ship had lightened up enough to clear the reefs and sail on to the safety of the open sea. Perhaps it had made a few hundred yards of headway and then come to grief on another reef. Perhaps the storm had broken the ship apart, sending different sections to float away to different destinations. Perhaps the ship had made it all the way home to England or Spain or France or Holland. Unless the finder decided to spend the time and lavish sums of money to search naval archives and mount a proper underwater expedition, no one would ever be sure of the ship's fate.

One day, while Teddy was examining a stretch of reef, I returned to the cannons. I was going to fan away the sand at the base of the heap of encrusted iron. I hoped to find some small telltale sign of a wreck. Maybe an emerald ring or a gold chain. Something modest.

The water was clear and the visibility seemingly endless. The cannons were in plain sight from the surface forty or fifty feet away. I remember the pile as being higher than I was tall and twenty-five or thirty feet long. A friend of ours was snorkeling on the surface. He waved to me as I sank to the bottom. I began to creep along the sand, fanning with my hand here and there. I couldn't wait to expose a crack that might be hiding what had, by now, become in my mind the Gem of Gems.

After a few pleasant but fruitless minutes of fanning, I heard a smacking sound from above. I looked up and saw that my snorkeling friend was slapping the surface and pointing down at me—or so it appeared. I looked at him for a moment, to be sure that he wasn't in trouble. Then I waved at him and continued on my way.

The slapping stopped, and now I heard the sound of swim fins churning through the water. I looked up and saw the snorkeler swimming—no, *racing*—toward the boat. He'd become bored, I assumed, or cold (though the water was soup warm). I kept going.

Not till much later did I learn that what he had been doing with all his noisy slapping was trying to save my life.

From his prospect high above, he had a clear view of the entire area: not just the cannons, but the sand plains that spread out from them on all sides. Seconds after I had begun to creep along the sand, he had seen, emerging from the gloom on the opposite side of the cannons, a great white shark. Not a big one—ten or twelve feet at most, probably a young male—but a great white shark nonetheless.

Anyone who has ever seen a great white in the water will never mistake it for any other species of shark. Seen from above, the great white has a unique profile. Its hefty, jumbo-jet fuselage is distinguished by what's called its caudal fin. The caudal fin is a curved horizontal fin that sticks out just before the tail on both sides of its body. It gives support to the tail, and streamlines the shark. Caudal fins exist in billfish and a few other species of sharks, but in none are they so large and noticeable. Seen from the side, a great white is thicker and more robust than, say, a silky. Its snout is perfectly proportioned, not as sharp as a mako's, not as blunt as a tiger shark's. Seen head-on, a great white is broad-shouldered and neckless. Its lower jaw stays slightly open, showing grabbing and tearing teeth. Its upper lip looks puckery, as if the upper jaw were toothless. It isn't really, of course. The upper jaw is home to row upon row of big, serrated triangular cutting teeth that lie relaxed, nearly horizontal, against the upper gums.

Seen from anywhere, it is a *big* shark, long and bulky— a seventeen-foot female can weigh over two tons. And it moves with the ease and confidence of the toughest dude on the block.

My friend the snorkeler had been with us in South Australia, and he knew what he was seeing.

He told me later that from his vantage point the pile of cannons looked like an almond. He could see me swimming along the right side of the almond and the shark swimming up the left side at approximately the same speed. He calculated that the shark and I would meet at the point of the almond, as precisely as two characters in a Warner Bros. cartoon. He had slapped the water to warn me and pointed not at me but at the shark. Suddenly the thought had occurred to him that causing a ruckus on the surface might possibly attract the shark up to him. He figured that I at least had the advantage of being completely submerged and on apparently equal turf with the shark. But floundering on the surface, he was nothing but bait. So he departed, hastily, for the boat.

In my judgment, he did exactly the correct thing.

I, meanwhile, continued. I was oblivious to everything except the phantom jewels undoubtedly nestled in the next pocket of sand between cannons, or certainly the one after that. My eyes riveted on the bottom, I had no reason to look up.

I reached the end of the pile of cannons, the point of the almond. Then I did look up, to orient myself, and at that very moment the great white reached the same spot.

We saw each other. Our eyes locked for perhaps a nanosecond. It was just long enough for my brain to register and recognize what my eyes were seeing. I guess its brain registered shock and surprise.

I was paralyzed. The shark wasn't. It braked with its pectoral fins, like a plane with its flaps down for landing. Then it spun completely around in its own length and vanished in a billowy cloud of brown, which had exploded from its bowel.

I was alone, kneeling on the bottom, stunned and breathless. And within a few seconds, I was covered by a cloud of great-white-shark crap.

11

You Say You *Want* to Dive with Sharks?

Well, you'd better be with an experienced scuba diver.

And you'd better be guided by a veteran dive master who knows the local waters and its inhabitants very well indeed. Because the sharks of one area may behave completely differently from sharks *of the same exact species* that inhabit another area.

And you'd better be prepared to expect the unexpected and act accordingly.

And you'd better be *extremely* lucky, unless you are in areas where feeding stations have been established and the sharks are used to having humans in the water with them. In those places sharks have come to associate humans with (not *as*) food. Everywhere else, sharks have no interest at all in hanging out with humans. In fact, sharks go out of their way to avoid us—especially scuba divers.

Scuba divers appear to a shark to be large, strange (they look like no other animal it knows), alien (they emit blasts of bubbles), noisy (those bubbles are *loud*), possibly threatening, and definitely unappetizing.

More and more these days, at dive sites, hotels, and resorts around the world, divers want to see, be in the presence of, and photograph sharks. They're prepared to travel vast distances and pay big money to dive with sharks of all kinds, from great whites to whale sharks, blue sharks, hammerheads, duskies, and silkies.

Every year millions of sharks are killed for their fins. Crusaders who want to save sharks have worked hard to come up with a statistic proving that a live shark is worth much more to a community than a dead one. The following statistic may not be reliable, but it makes the point: every shark killed for its fins brings a fisherman and his community somewhere between five and fifty dollars. But every shark that is left alive to become an attraction for diving tourists generates fifty thousand dollars a year in income for the community.

While that statistic isn't provable, there is an underlying truth to it: tourism is the fastest-growing industry in the world. Tourism can help save ailing, inefficient economies. Since diving is an important part of tourism, and divers want to see sharks, that makes sharks a lot more valuable alive than dead.

Conclusion: preserve your local sharks and you'll attract tourist dollars. Those dollars ripple out into the rest of the island (or seaside or port or coastline) economy. They support restaurants, hotels, car-rental franchises, shops, video-rental stores, and so on.

For the most part, intentional diving with sharks is reasonably safe, because it is chaperoned and supervised by experts. Even the many shark-feeding enterprises that are springing up all over the world (especially in the Bahamas) are, as a rule, conducted so that the paying customers are kept safe.

Shark feeding, however, is increasingly controversial. Scientists worry that behavioral patterns are changed in sharks that become used to being fed by humans. Natural behavior becomes unnatural when it is interfered with. Sharks lose part of their "sharkness."

Surfers, abalone divers, chambers of commerce, and seaside merchants are worried about a different possible problem—and a more practical one. If certain sharks learn to associate humans with food, how will they react to humans who *don't* come bearing food? To counter that concern, operators of shark-feeding programs point out that the sharks conditioned to eat at feeding stations tend to remain in those areas. If you make your living hunting for food and you find a place where food is given to you, why move? The sharks that occasionally maul people in the surf off beaches aren't reacting to conditioning; they're chasing food.

I can't speak with authority to the scientists' concern, though it sounds logical and serious. But I am intimately

The first great white shark I ever saw underwater.
South Australia, 1974.

Shark's view of me in a cage. Do I look tasty?
I don't think so.

The shark approaches the cage and
prepares to take a test bite.

After completing a circle of the cage, the shark comes at
it from a different angle and lifts its head out of the
water to swallow some bait.

The shark has snagged in its teeth the rope connecting the cage to the boat. In the cage, armed only with my trusty broomstick, I realize I'm in trouble.

On the beach set of *Jaws* in the cold spring of 1974. Director Steven Spielberg prepares me for my scene as a television reporter.

"Bruce," the mechanical shark that was a miracle of mid-1970s technology.

Left to right: My wife, Wendy; me; actor Roy Scheider (Chief Brody in the movie); and, in front of me, our then five-year-old son, Clayton.

A family dive in Florida, December 1995. Left to right: Wendy, Christopher (age eight), the dive master, and me.

My son Clayton (age eleven); wife, Wendy; and daughter, Tracy (age thirteen), in Bermuda, 1980.

A Galápagos sea lion playing with my ten-year-old son Christopher's fins in November 1997.

One of the most memorable shows (for me) from ABC's *The American Sportsman*. Unaware that I'm leaking blood from a wound in my ankle, I've become an object of desire for an oceanic whitetip. My broomstick is about to meet its end.

Riding a giant manta ray in the Sea of Cortez for ABC's
The American Sportsman. A magical experience in my life.

Stan Waterman, one of America's pioneer divers and
underwater filmmakers, greeting—while attempting to film—
a whale shark, the biggest fish in the sea.

An armada of scalloped hammerheads in the Sea of Cortez.
No one knows for certain why they gather in such numbers—
perhaps it's a breeding ritual—but they seem to have
no interest in human beings.

One of several species of bull shark—
unpredictable and dangerous.

A silvertip in the South Pacific—a gorgeous shark
that is being heavily overfished.

A mako shark, one of the fastest fish in the sea.

A blue shark—another species that has been devastated by overfishing.

A tiger shark—big, robust, and dangerous.

A curious moray eel slides out of its hole.

A stingray comes in for a landing at "Stingray City" at Grand Cayman Island in March 1999. This was Christopher's first successful underwater photograph, taken when he had just turned twelve years old.

A great white shark that circled our tiny boat several times off Gansbaai, South Africa, in 1999. When we boarded the boat, the captain said, "Rule number one: if anybody falls overboard and a shark grabs him, the person next to him jumps down onto the shark's head. That startles 'im and makes 'im let go. Usually."

The most notorious face in nature: a great white shark, upper jaw dropped into "bite position." In fact, though, this was a moment of curiosity, not attack. The shark had poked its head out of the water and was just having a look around. South Africa, 1999.

Nature's perfect creation: a great white shark, the largest of all the meat-eating fish in the sea.

familiar with the more practical problem. I was part of a shark "experiment" long ago. The memory of it, seen with the benefit of hindsight over many years of acquired knowledge and experience, does disturb me.

Shark feeding as a resort attraction was fairly new in the mid-1970s. Scuba diving itself was still a relatively young and exotic sport. I was asked to do a TV show on Long Island in the Bahamas. A dive master there had conditioned local sharks to assemble at a certain sand hole in a reef at a certain time of day. The sharks expected and accepted food skewered on a spear stuck in the sand. Sometimes they ate directly from his hands.

The routine called for paying customers to gather in a circle in the sand hole, surrounding the dive master, who would lure the sharks to the food. The sharks would arrive, swooping over and between the divers, and would then fight over the food. After ten or fifteen minutes, the food would be gone and the sharks would leave. The sharks would also eyeball the divers and pass near enough to give them a thrill and a chance to take a good close-up with their underwater cameras.

Not for us. Not exciting enough. We were pros. We had to go where other divers dared not go. We had to test the limits. So somebody cooked up the idea of measuring the bite dynamics of the sharks. We wanted to measure how many pounds of pressure per square inch a shark—in this case, a variety of bull shark—could exert with its jaws.

We built a gnathodynamometer—a seventeen-letter word

for a bite meter. It was nothing more than a sandwich of two dead fish tied to a slab of pressure-sensitive plastic. The idea was that the "talent"—a photogenic young Ph.D. candidate named Clarisse and I—would hand-feed the sandwich to as many sharks as possible. Then we would measure, from the depth of the tooth marks, the pressure the sharks' jaws had exerted.

The first gnathodynamometer was an instant casualty. No one had paused to consider what would happen if two, three, or more sharks went for it at once. Clarisse and I held it out to a single shark. The shark swam between us, opened its mouth, seized the sandwich, and was instantly dive-bombed by three other sharks. Knocked aside, we watched helplessly as the sharks swarmed in a ball of fury, tore the fish to shreds, and swam away with the plastic.

We tried again, this time while a dive master distracted most of the sharks with their usual food. One shark detached from the group, cruised over the bottom toward us, and lunged upward for the gnathodynamometer. But its tail disturbed so much sand, which billowed in a cloud around us, that it couldn't see where it was going. Instead of biting the sandwich, it grabbed a yellow steel-cased strobe light and gnawed away until it was convinced that the light wasn't appetizing. Then it gave up and swam off.

It took several days of trial and error for us to get the shots we wanted. But we succeeded at last, without losing any fingers or limbs. My eleven-year-old son, Clayton, had watched the action through a face mask at the surface. When the shooting was over, he asked his mother and me to take him down to see a shark—if any were still around.

Without thinking, Wendy and I said, "Sure." Clayton had been diving for three years. He was careful and knowledgeable, and he obeyed instructions. We knew that most of the sharks had gone. We were confident that between us we could shepherd him safely to and from the bottom.

We checked his gear, refreshed him on all the precautions, and went overboard off the stern. I went first and sank straight to the bottom; Clayton came next; Wendy followed.

We three knelt on the sand and looked around at the empty blue, hoping to see a single shark swimming calmly in the distance.

We never saw the first shark arrive. It bore down on us from above, passed quickly before us, and began to circle ten, perhaps fifteen, feet away.

Two more sharks arrived and joined the circle. Wendy and I closed in on Clayton and looked into each other's eyes. We knew at once the terrible mistake we had just made. By jumping into the water and going down into the same sand hole where the feeding ritual took place every day, we had given cues to conditioned animals. And they had responded.

Three more sharks swam in from the gloom. Other gray shadows began to appear in the distance.

Soon there were thirteen sharks circling us, expecting a meal but calm . . . at least for the time being.

We had no food to give them. We couldn't hold up our end of the bargain.

How long would it take the first shark to understand that it had been betrayed, that the rules had been broken? How would it react?

Were they all well fed? Had one or two perhaps not gotten their share during the feeding?

All I knew for certain was that we had no time to wait for answers. Already a couple of the sharks were showing signs of . . . not agitation, not excitement . . . the only word that came to me was *impatience*.

One shark shivered visibly; a ripple traveled the length of its hard, sleek, steel gray body. Another began to swim in spurts, speeding up and slowing down.

I couldn't tell what Clayton was feeling. He knelt motionless, now and then turning his head to watch a particular shark. Mostly he let the parade pass before his eyes. Wendy and I had a hand on each of his arms, as one of us always did in any remotely scary circumstance. We wanted to be sure that he wouldn't, in panic, suddenly rush for the surface, forgetting his training. Then he would risk becoming a victim of any one of several unhappy accidents.

I looked up at the boat, which was clearly visible some thirty feet directly overhead. Then I made eye contact with Wendy and told her (as best I could) that I had come to a decision and that she should do exactly as I did. She seemed to—and indeed, she did—understand.

I tapped Clayton to get his attention. He looked up at me, obviously excited, obviously afraid. His eyes, seen through the distortion of mask and water, were the size of extra-large eggs. I made the "okay" sign to him—a circle formed by thumb and forefinger—then touched his mask and mine. I was saying, *Watch me, do as I do.* He shot me the "okay" sign.

Together, we three rose from our knees and stood on the sand.

The sharks noticed our movement. Though they didn't change their pace, they closed ranks just a bit, shrinking the circle.

Wendy and I faced each other and flanked Clayton. My right hand held her left. With my left hand, I mimed counting down from three to zero. She closed her eyes for a second, then nodded.

I counted down. At zero we filled our lungs with compressed air, pressed the purge valves on our regulator mouthpieces, and kicked off the bottom.

A thick, noisy column of bubbles filled the space between us. We shielded Clayton with our bodies as we rose toward the boat. We exhaled slowly, fighting the urge to hurry, staying always beneath the last of our bubbles, to prevent any rogue air bubble from being trapped in some tiny space in our lungs. If that happens, the air bubble can burst free and travel to your heart or brain, where it might kill you.

My tactic was simple and by no means guaranteed to

succeed. In general, sharks don't like bubbles. In general, they stay away from loud, erratic bursts of bubbles. Engineers have built bubble "curtains" in attempts to protect beaches, but they've proven to be unreliable.

My hope was that by huddling together and blasting bubbles from our regulators, we would look to the sharks like a horrible machine. I hoped we would not even rate a close inspection, let alone an exploratory bite.

Not once did I look down. But Clayton did, and later he told me that the circle of sharks had broken apart as soon as we left and that individual sharks had begun to follow us upward.

We broke through the surface, and in a single motion Wendy and I propelled Clayton up onto the swim step. Next Wendy hauled herself onto the little platform. I hung off, prepared to kick at any shark that made a run at her legs.

One shark had followed us nearly to the surface. Now it circled tightly just below my feet. I couldn't turn away to climb aboard the boat. I had to keep watching it, in case it should lunge for me.

I hoped that hands would reach down from above and haul me aboard, and Wendy did, in fact, grab the neck of my tank to keep me from drifting away. But she didn't have the strength to lift me and my tank and weights and wet suit clear of the water.

After perhaps a minute, the shark turned away and swam off, and I shucked my tank and pulled myself into the boat.

Wendy and I looked at our son. He had taken off his tank and was shedding his wet suit. He was trembling, and his lips were blue from cold or fear.

We had no words for each other. We had almost lost . . . We could have lost . . . We were both guilty of . . . How could we have . . . ?

"Wow!" Clayton shouted. "I've never been so scared in my life."

"I know," I began. "I—"

"Can I go again? Can I? Please?"

We said no.

12
Some Shark Facts and a Story

Whether you are fascinated by sharks or dinosaurs, you have to admit that sharks have one particular advantage over dinosaurs: they still exist. They're still visible in the wild, still around to be photographed, filmed, and videotaped. The Discovery Channel's *Shark Week* has become a popular and successful institution. Most broadcast and cable TV channels have access to a huge archive of shark footage. Digital technology nowadays is so good that as soon as discoveries of any kind are made—whether of new species or new behaviors—they're recorded and broadcast to large audiences. The movie *Jaws* appears on television somewhere in the world nearly every day of the year, and it continues to draw audiences.

Still, it's possible that some readers of this book don't know much about sharks. So for them, and for their parents and teachers, here is a brief primer on sharks. These are "true facts," without hype, gore, or sensation:

✛ Sharks are fish, but they're not like other fish, because they have no bones. Sharks and the other members of the elasmobranch family of sea creatures, including skates and rays, have skeletons made of cartilage. Cartilage is the same stuff we have in our knees and other joints and in our noses and ears.

✛ Sharks are some of the oldest animals on earth. They've been around much longer than man or any other mammal—probably close to four hundred million years. And they haven't changed very much in at least the last thirty million years because they haven't had to: they've always efficiently performed the functions nature programmed them to do: eat, swim, and reproduce.

✛ There are hundreds of different kinds of sharks. Nobody knows exactly how many because (1) new species are being discovered all the time, and (2) we have explored very little of the ocean, which covers 70 percent of our planet's surface. We really have no notion of the true nature and variety of all that lives down there.

✛ Sharks range over all extremes of size, appearance, and appetite. They include the whale shark, the biggest fish in the sea. Whale sharks can grow to fifty feet long and weigh many tons, but they are completely harmless to people and eat only the tiniest of sea creatures. They also include the cookie-cutter shark, which grows to only about a foot and a half. But cookie-cutter sharks inflict terrible wounds on much bigger animals, like other sharks and dolphins, by using their razor-sharp teeth to remove large chunks of flesh.

✛ Sharks include the largest meat-eating fish in the sea—the great white, which has attacked and eaten human beings. Some of the smallest meat eaters are sharks, too, like the so-called cigar shark, which fits in the palm of your hand, and the dwarf shark, which only grows to ten inches long.

✛ Sharks include some of the weirdest-looking fish in the sea. The horn shark, which grows to roughly three feet long, has a face that resembles a pig's and flat teeth—not pointed—that it uses to crush the animals it eats. The wobbegong shark is camouflaged to be invisible against a coral reef. It never bothers people . . . unless people bother it. A friend of mine was bitten by a wobbegong when she put her finger on it to show me how well it was hidden.

✛ Sharks are very important to maintaining the balance of nature in the sea. As apex predators, they keep other animals healthy and in check, culling populations of the old, the weak, and the sick.

✛ Scientists suspect that sharks perform several other important functions in the sea. But they don't know exactly what those functions are because they've had so little time and money with which to study sharks. Unlike whales, sharks do not breathe air, do not nurse their young, do not communicate with one another in an audible "language," and do not interrelate with humans at all. Consequently, people can't easily identify with sharks, and there has not been much popular effort to get to know them.

✝ Since the first human ventured onto the sea thousands of years ago, sharks have always been perceived as danger-ous, sometimes even evil. So there hasn't been much pressure on governments to spend money to study them. Most people believe that the best way to deal with sharks is to stay away from them. Some even believe that the only good shark is a dead shark, a belief that springs from a combination of fear and ignorance.

✝ Unfortunately, sharks have turned out to be very vulnerable to destruction, and possibly even extinction, at the hands of humans. Sharks are prized for their fins (for soup), their meat (especially makos), their skins (for leather), their teeth (for jewelry), and their organs and cartilage (for medi-cines). Sharks have in recent years been so heavily over-fished that some species may never recover.

✝ The downfall of sharks may, ironically, be accelerated by the same qualities that have made them so well adapted for so many millions of years. Because apex predators are at the top of the food chain, nothing preys on sharks except larger versions of themselves and, sometimes, killer whales. To maintain ecological balance, the number of each species of apex predator—be it grizzly bear, lion, tiger, or shark—must remain low. These animals breed late in life and not too often, and produce few young that will survive to adulthood.

Great white sharks, for example, have small litters (often only one or two). But each pup is born large (four or five feet long), fully formed, fully armed, and ready to rumble. Other species may pup many live young, but they're so small and vulnerable to being eaten by other creatures that only the fittest (and the luckiest) survive.

In their appearance, their efficiency, and the striking evidence of their incredible adaptability, sharks are—to me, anyway—among the most beautiful creatures on earth.

We are all—each living thing on the planet—linked together in the complex chain of life. Here is a story I wrote about sharks, to explain how they function in that chain.

THE DAY ALL THE SHARKS DIED

Once upon a time, there was a seaside village whose people lived in harmony with nature.

They made their living from the sea. They caught fish on the reef that protected the village from the full fury of ocean storms. They gathered clams and oysters, mussels and scallops from the bays and coves and inlets. Some they ate themselves. Some they sold to people in other towns and villages, from whom they bought necessities like lightbulbs and clothing and radios and refrigerators and fuel for their boats and cars.

Their biggest business, which employed the most people and brought in the most money, was lobster fishing. Lobstermen owned special boats and had special licenses that permitted them to set a certain number of pots or traps to catch lobsters. The law permitted the fishermen to catch only lobsters that were too big to pass through a special ring, which meant that they were old enough to have bred and had young of their own. Smaller lobsters were put back in the sea to live and grow, as were female lobsters carrying eggs.

Everyone worked together to maintain a healthy, stable population of lobsters, for many people's livelihoods depended on them. First there were the fishermen who caught them, the mates who worked on the boats, and the wholesalers on the docks who bought the lobsters, processed them, and packed them up for shipping. Then there were the truckers who took the lobsters to stores and restaurants up and down the coast. There were the men and women who worked at the restaurants where lobsters were served, the businesses that cleaned the linen used in the restaurants, and the bankers who financed the businesses. On it went, like ripples spreading from the splash of a stone dropped in a pond.

A small colony of sea lions lived on a rocky point of land that joined the breakwater at the mouth of the harbor. In the springtime tourists from other towns would come to the village and have lunch at one of the restaurants on the harbor. They came just for the fun of watching the newborn sea lion pups playing with one another, or learning how to swim and hunt for food, or sunning themselves on the warm rocks.

The villagers did not think much, or worry at all, about the great number and variety of creatures that lived in the sea. The sea and all its living things seemed infinite, indestructible, eternal.

Nor did they worry about the predators that lived in the sea. They knew that sharks patrolled the reef and the deep water beyond. But never—not in living memory or in village lore—had anyone ever been bitten, let alone killed, by a shark.

The villagers had, of course, been taught from birth to respect the sea and the animals in it, so they took sensible precautions. Even on the scorching hot days of summer no one swam at dawn or at dusk, when sharks were known to feed on the reef. At those times, once in a great while, a dorsal fin could be spotted slicing the flat-calm surface of the water in the harbor.

They never swam near fishermen, or wherever bait was in the water. They never swam if they saw fish feeding or birds feeding on fish. No one swam or snorkeled or dove with a fresh cut or an open sore.

Nobody fished for sharks because none of the locals liked shark meat and there wasn't a market for it anywhere nearby. If a fisherman caught a shark by accident, on a line or in a net, he'd let it go. Nobody in the village ever killed anything just for the sake of killing.

One day people noticed a big boat—big enough, in fact, to be considered a ship—lingering not far offshore. Smaller boats were put overboard from the ship, and they cruised up and down the reef.

Village fishermen who had gotten close enough

to the ship to read its name couldn't remember it or pronounce it. It was stenciled on the ship's bow and fantail not only in a foreign language but also in an alphabet nobody could decipher.

The one peculiar thing about the ship that fishermen could describe was that on her stern were two very, very big—gigantic, even—spools. Each spool looked like it could hold at least a mile's worth of thick, strong fishing line. And visible in the coils of line were hooks, too many to count.

When the people in the village awoke on the morning of the third day, the ship was gone. Everything seemed to be okay; nothing looked different.

There was no way anyone could know that, over the past two days, their village had been assaulted.

The first sign that something was wrong was discovered by fishermen who went out to the reef. Scattered over the bottom, in the reef and on the sand, they saw the dead bodies of sharks. (Because sharks do not have swim bladders like other fish, when they die they do not float. They sink to the bottom.) They saw that the sharks had not only been killed, they had also been mutilated. Their fins had been slashed off—dorsal fins from their backs, caudal fins from their tails, pectoral fins from their sides—and the sharks had been thrown back into the sea to bleed to death or drown.

The fishermen's first reaction was anger: so *this* was what the foreign ship had been doing offshore, killing sharks and taking their fins to sell to the people who make shark-fin soup, an expensive delicacy.

Their second reaction was frustration. What

could they do about this thievery? They knew the answer: nothing. The ship had come from a foreign land. From experience the villagers knew that their local police and wardens and marshals had no power over foreign vessels.

Their third reaction was resignation. Well, the shark populations will rebound. Sharks from other regions up and down the coast will come here. Nature will stay in balance.

What they didn't know was that there were almost no sharks in other regions up and down the coast. The big ship and the boats it carried had worked the entire coastline. It had taken nearly all the sharks from all the reefs and used the long lines on the huge spools that sat on the stern of the big boat to catch the open-water sharks, the big ones that fed on sea lions.

For the first few weeks, nothing seemed much different. Fish and lobsters were caught and sold, money was earned and money was spent, and life continued as before.

Then fishermen began to notice that they were catching fewer lobsters in the pots. Slowly at first, then more rapidly, the number of lobsters was declining. Often lobster fishermen found in their pots not lobsters but octopuses. They had never paid attention to octopuses before. Now the octopuses seemed to be everywhere.

Within a month or two, the villagers realized that the number of sea lions had increased, too, especially young ones. As the sea lion population grew, the number of fish caught by the village's fishermen declined. In itself, this was no mystery. Sea lions eat fish, so as their numbers increased, they took more and more fish from the sea.

The mystery was, why had the sea lion population exploded?

Soon there were so many sea lions that they outgrew their rocky point and spread back toward the village. Some took up residence on docks, some on boats moored in the harbor. Since sea lions poop wherever they please, boat owners found the decks and cockpits of their boats soiled and stinking.

When the wind blew toward shore, the stink wafted into the village and made dining an unpleasant experience. Restaurants lost customers. Waiters and waitresses were laid off, and some had to move away to find new jobs, leaving houses and apartments vacant.

Lobster catches continued to drop. Most lobster fishermen had borrowed money from banks to pay for their boats. Some had borrowed to pay for their homes as well. Now, with their income so low, they couldn't make the monthly loan payments. Eventually the banks had no choice but to take the lobster boats from the fishermen and try to sell them to someone somewhere else.

Every one of these decisions and actions became a new stone dropped into the pond. Ripples spread, affecting businesses and men and women and their families for miles and miles around.

And always the question lingered: *why?* What had gone so terribly wrong so terribly fast?

By the time the answer came the following

summer, the village was in trouble. The signs were visible to anyone. The words FOR SALE were printed, stenciled, painted, and scribbled, and hung on houses, boats, shops, restaurants, cars in driveways, and lawn mowers on lawns. The streets were silent, the harbor nearly empty. And the vast, uncountable population of sea lions now inhabited every square inch of waterfront property in the village.

All the sea lions were unnaturally lean. Only those strong enough to swim far out to sea and dive very deep to find fish were able to feed themselves. Even they spent so much energy catching food that they could barely keep themselves nourished; they had no extra to feed to their young. Their natural duty was to keep themselves alive so they could breed new litters of pups every year. And so, as nature had programmed them to do, mother sea lions let their pups starve. The bodies of the dead young sea lions rotted on the rocks and washed around in the shallows.

It was a high school student working on a paper who discovered what had hurt the village, and her discovery wasn't even very complicated. It was just a matter of knowing where to look.

The student examined the food chain in the sea when the village had been thriving. At the top were the sharks. Some sharks preyed on the fish on the reef; all sharks preyed on octopuses. Octopuses, in fact, were one of the sharks' favorite foods. That was one of the things that kept octopuses from overrunning the reef. Octopuses lay thousands and thousands of eggs at one time, because not many usually survive. When the sharks disappeared, the student discovered, the octopus population had boomed out of natural proportion.

Now, one of an octopus's favorite foods is lobster. An octopus will trap a lobster with one or more of its eight powerful arms, squeeze it to death and crack it apart with its arms, and then eat it with its powerful beak. Even small octopuses can catch and eat small lobsters. So when the sea around the village became overpopulated with octopuses, the lobster population suddenly crashed.

Very soon there were no more lobsters for the fishermen to catch.

Normally, other sharks—larger ones, including great whites—preyed upon the sea lion colony. They took the weak, the sick, the malformed, and the vulnerable, leaving only the strong and healthy sea lions to maintain the colony.

When those sharks were killed by the big fishing ship, there were no predators left to control the growth of the sea lion colony. And sharks are not only predators but scavengers as well. So even the dead sea lions were not recycled into the food chain but were left to rot and become host to flies and other carriers of disease.

The most discouraging discovery the student made was that there was a possibility that the village might never recover. No one could know for certain, but there was a chance that the marine food chain had been altered forever.

✢ ✢ ✢ ✢

A year passed, and another, and then, one day, a couple on a sailboat just beyond the reef saw a dark triangular fin slice through the calm water. A few feet behind it, a tall tail fin swished back and forth. It was a shark, a big one, and whereas a few years earlier the couple might have shuddered at the sight of the fins, now they cheered.

Soon other sharks began to visit the reef, and gradually—very gradually—the number of sea lions declined. So did the number of octopuses, and that meant that more lobsters had a chance to survive to adulthood. By the time the high school student had finished college, lobstermen could once again make a living from the waters around the village.

What had saved the village was an idea hatched by some scientists alarmed by the decline in the number of fish in all the oceans of the world. Too many boats with too much modern technology were taking too many fish from the sea too quickly for many species to recover. The idea the scientists had was to locate areas where fish were breeding and spending their first few months of life and to protect them from fishing.

It took them a long time and a lot of arguing and pleading, but eventually they were given permission to create what came to be called Marine Protected Areas in many places around the world.

One of the MPAs was located a few miles offshore, up the coast from the village. As animal populations in the protected area recovered, their eggs and larvae drifted south and began to nourish the reefs and waters near the village.

Some people resisted MPAs. They believed they should be allowed to fish for whatever they wanted wherever and whenever they wanted and with the most effective killing equipment available. They argued that they had to feed their families *now*, and they couldn't afford to worry about the future.

Millions of others, however—and their numbers grew—recognized that if random, destructive fishing was permitted to continue, someday there would be no oceans. Instead, there could be a catastrophic collapse of marine life, and along with that would surely come a human catastrophe.

They couldn't let that happen.

And neither can we.

III

13
Dangerous to Man?
Moray Eels, Killer Whales, Barracudas, and Other Creatures We Fear

We humans live on the edge of the world's largest primal wilderness, the ocean. We venture onto and into it for recreation, relaxation, and exercise. But we don't appreciate the fact that the ocean is the hunting ground for most of the living things on planet Earth.

No matter how peaceful the sea may seem on a warm and sunny day, it is in fact always—*always!*—a brutal world. Two basic rules govern it: kill or be killed, and eat or be eaten.

Sharks are by no means the only predators that haunt the wilds outside our door. They're just the biggest and most spectacular. Every living thing, of every size and shape conceivable, possesses weapons with which to defend itself and tools with which to feed itself. When we enter alien territory, we can startle, frighten, or, occasionally, tempt creatures that are minding their own business and behaving as nature has programmed them to behave. So we shouldn't be surprised if we get into trouble.

Many years ago, Roger Caras wrote a book I liked titled *Dangerous to Man*. In it he examined many of the animals we see as threatening to humans. He explained why and in what circumstances each one should or shouldn't be feared. His premise, of course, was that no animal is dangerous to humans if humans leave it alone. Some friends and I believed that Caras's book could be translated into an excellent series of informative half hours for television. We almost succeeded in getting the project made. It was not to be, but the premise of the book is still valid. In the next pages I'll describe the marine animals most commonly thought of as being dangerous to humans. I hope you'll conclude, as I have, that the animals *truly* most dangerous to humans are humans.

The list that follows is incomplete. I've included only the animals that I or friends of mine have personal knowledge of, or animals I've studied for so long that I think I know them pretty well. (For technical details about some of the creatures, I have borrowed from Richard Ellis's superb *Encyclopedia of the Sea*.)

MORAY EELS

There are a great many kinds, colors, and sizes of moray eels. Most of them live in tropical and subtropical waters.

Morays range in size from under a foot to nearly ten feet long. I know from experience that a seven-footer—as big around as a football and displaying its long, white, needle-like fangs—is as scary-looking a monster as there is underwater.

One of the things that makes a moray look so frightening is the way it breathes. Its mouth opens and closes constantly, which forces oxygen-rich water over its gills. But this, combined with its wide, blank, maniacally staring eyes, makes the eel look as if it can't wait to rip your head off.

Morays aren't poisonous, but their bites can carry so much toxic bacteria that they might as well be. They're scavengers as well as predators, and they will eat rotten flesh. A moray bite is usually ragged (thus difficult to sew up), exceedingly painful, and quick to become infected. It is also usually a mistake: the eel confuses a human finger or toe for a piece of food. Usually, that is. But not always.

David Doubilet is an excellent underwater photographer with whom I've worked for more than twenty years. He was once severely bitten on the hand by a yellowish moray off Hawaii. The eel, he says, literally charged him. It zoomed out of its hole, bit him, and went home. The wound not only took forever to heal but also did considerable damage to David's hand.

Al Giddings, the underwater cinematographer who worked on *Titanic* and *The Abyss,* was bitten by a moray in 1976. This happened during the filming of the movie based on my novel *The Deep*. Columbia Pictures had built a two-million-gallon tank to contain its underwater sets in Bermuda. They stocked it with live animals, including a shark and some eels. One of the eels took a liking to one of Al's toes. Al kept his toe, but the wound became infected immediately, and he lost some diving time.

There's no reason for swimmers, snorkelers, or scuba divers to get into trouble with morays. And there are only a couple of circumstances in which people do get bitten.

The eels live in small caves, crannies, and holes in reefs. A diver who goes poking around—searching for lobsters, perhaps—risks having a probing hand mistaken for a fish, seized, gnawed on, and shredded.

Another risky business involves morays that have been conditioned to accept and be fed by humans. As dive masters and other sea-savvy folks know, conditioning is not the same as taming. Eels, fish, sharks, and other marine creatures (except for some of the mammals) *cannot be tamed.* No one should ever try to treat a moray eel like a pet.

The danger in conditioning morays is rarely to the conditioner or the conditioner's customers. They, after all, play by established rules. They arrive at the dive site, bringing fish scraps or other tasty dead things for the eel. The eel emerges from its hole, expecting to be fed. It is fed, and it permits itself to be touched and handled. Sometimes it will hunt for morsels concealed on the diver's body. Then it will slither in and out of the diver's buoyancy-compensator vest, between his legs, or around his neck.

For the paying customer, the performance looks truly impressive, and, in fact, it is.

The most remarkable morays I've ever seen lived on a reef off Grand Cayman. They had been conditioned by Wayne and Ann Hasson, who at the time ran a successful diving operation in the Cayman Islands. (You'll have noticed by now that I keep using the word *conditioned* instead of *trained*. It's because I'm not certain that what the eels are taught to do is really training. They don't jump through hoops or play volleyball or do anything else they're not used to doing. They eat—though, granted, in an unnatural way. That is, they eat from the hands of humans, whom they have been taught to tolerate and, to an extent, trust. Is that training? I don't think so. I think it's conditioning.)

Wayne and Ann worked with the two green morays they named Waldo and Waldeen. Both were enormous: six and a half or seven feet long (longer than I am tall, that much I know for sure). They were at least a foot high, and as thick as a large honeydew or a small watermelon.

David Doubilet and I were doing a story on the Caymans for *National Geographic*. Wendy and our then fourteen-year-old daughter, Tracy—both certified divers—had come along to enjoy a couple of weeks of the best diving in the Caribbean.

Tracy has always had a mystical, almost spooky, ability to communicate with animals. I don't mean "communicate" in the Dr. Dolittle sense; she doesn't talk to animals. She and animals merely appear to trust each other.

That kind of trust isn't uncommon for humans to have with dogs, cats, horses, and other mammals. But with *fish*? I have seen big groupers come to Tracy—while avoiding every other human in the area—and almost snuggle up to her. I'll forever remember seeing her in the Caymans, walking slowly along the bottom, with two groupers swimming beside her, one under each arm.

Valerie Taylor is the only person I know with a greater affinity than Tracy for marine creatures. Valerie is the legendary Australian photographer, diver, and marine conservationist. She truly is spooky—off the scale. I believe that Valerie could wordlessly convince any fish, eel, or dolphin to fetch her newspaper, pick up her laundry, and wash her car.

One day, Ann Hasson introduced Tracy to one of the giant green morays—Waldeen, I think. When the eel had been fed and stroked by Ann, it took immediately to Tracy. It snaked all around her, in and out of her buoyancy-compensator vest, seeming not to be seeking food so much as getting acquainted. Tracy never moved, except to raise her arms slowly to give Waldeen another platform to slither around.

After a few moments, the eel calmly slid away from Tracy and returned to its home in the reef. We all puttered around for another minute or two, then prepared to move on.

When I signaled to Tracy to follow us, however, she shook her head, calmly but definitely saying no.

I was bewildered: what did she mean, *no*? What did she plan to do, stand there all day? Then I saw her point downward with one index finger, and I looked at her feet. There was Waldeen, halfway out of the reef, with its huge, gaping jaws around Tracy's ankle. The eel's head was moving gently back and forth, its jaws throbbing open and closed on my daughter's bare flesh.

Waldeen was mouthing Tracy, the way a Labrador retriever will mouth your hand to get you to play with it. Labradors, though, are known for having a "soft mouth." Moray eels aren't.

Tracy's expression was serene. Clearly, she was neither hurt nor afraid. She stayed still. I stayed still, too, paralyzed with fear and wondering what I'd do if I suddenly vomited into my mask.

The eel played with Tracy's ankle for perhaps another thirty seconds, then withdrew into the reef.

We moved on.

When we returned to the Cayman Islands a couple of years later, I learned that both Waldo and Waldeen were gone. One had been caught and killed by local fishermen—illegally, of course—and the other was said to have vanished. I'd bet that he or she, whichever it was, had been killed, too. For the biggest danger in conditioning eels to trust humans is not to the humans but to the eels. Their fate is familiar and almost inevitable. I've seen it happen all over the world, from the Cayman Islands in the Caribbean to the Tuamotu Islands in French Polynesia.

An eel is conditioned to associate humans with food. Sometimes the betrayal is simple. A spearfisher will descend to the reef, maybe carrying food, maybe not. The eel will emerge from its den. The fisher kills it. More often, though, the eel's death is more complex.

Once there lived a big moray eel in a large coral head inside the lagoon of the Rangiroa Atoll in the Tuamotus. When our son Christopher was nine, he used to like to visit the eel, to watch it as it waited in ambush in the shelter of the coral. Now and then he'd see the eel dart out of its hole and, with blurring speed, snatch and kill a passing fish. Christopher kept his distance from the eel. Even though local laws forbade the feeding of morays, it was common knowledge that glass-bottom-boat operators from cruise ships would send snorkelers down with food. They would draw eels out of their holes for the entertainment of their passengers. Christopher didn't carry food with him, and he didn't want the eel to make any false assumptions about him.

News came one afternoon that a swimmer had been badly bitten by a moray eel and had had to be evacuated by air to a hospital in Tahiti. By coincidence, we were scheduled to go out into the lagoon that day. When we reached the coral head, Christopher put on mask, fins, and snorkel and dove down to see his friend the eel.

The eel had been speared, just behind the head. It was still alive, struggling to retreat into its hole. But the steel shaft that had gone clean through its body now stuck out a foot or more from either side, stopping the eel from retreating.

Christopher hung in the water, helpless, and watched the eel die.

We heard later what had happened. A snorkeler had happened by and seen the eel waiting in the opening of its hole. She had approached very close to the eel. The eel—thinking she was bringing food, like other humans who came so near—came out of its hole prepared to feed.

When the woman gave it nothing, the eel pursued her. It was conditioned to associate humans with food. The flesh the eel saw looked like food but was, in fact, the woman's hand.

I'm sure you can finish the story yourself. The eel was deemed too dangerous to live, and a diver was sent to kill it. In truth, of course, the eel had only been obeying the conditioning imprinted upon it by humans.

The single strangest experience I've ever had with moray eels occurred in the Galápagos Islands. I first went there in 1987 to appear in a television show for John Wilcox. Stan Waterman was one of two underwater cameramen. The other was Howard Hall, one of the finest wildlife filmmakers working anywhere in the world today. My "co-talent" was Paul Humann. Paul is the author of many fish-identification books and an expert still photographer who had spent hundreds, if not thousands, of hours underwater in the Galápagos. He would act as my guide and teacher for the cameras.

Before the simple two-week shoot was over, all three of them would escape death and serious injury by the narrowest of margins. Stan and Paul were lost in the open ocean at twilight and, another day, were set upon suddenly by a large school of very aggressive small sharks. One day Howard and Paul, after Stan and I had left, were in the boat we had chartered when it crashed into an island and sank in the middle of the night. (The boat had been running on automatic pilot, and the crewman on duty had only to watch the radar screen. He had been taught everything about the radar—except *what it was for*. He had gazed serenely as the blip indicating the island drew ever closer to the center of the screen, until finally the boat slammed head-on into the rocky shore.)

We had filmed sharks of several kinds, in situations both controlled and hairy. We had filmed tiny Galápagos penguins (the northernmost penguins in the world), which swam like miniature rockets in pursuit of their prey. We'd filmed exotic critters like red-lipped batfish, which looked like a medical experiment gone wrong, as if the body of a frog had been grafted onto the mouth of Mick Jagger. We had also filmed seals and iguanas, Sally Lightfoot crabs and blue-footed boobies.

What we hadn't yet filmed were moray eels. In the Galápagos they tend to congregate in large numbers in tight quarters. We had been told to expect to see four or five, or maybe more, eels poking out of a single hole, their heads jammed together, their jaws opening and closing as they breathed. We hadn't seen any yet, but we kept looking. We all knew it would make a wonderful image.

One day we found some—not once but several times—and it was wonderful and we filmed till we ran out of film. Then, as we turned away, we noticed something curious: the eels were following us. We were on a rough, open lava plain. From hidden holes all over the bottom, moray eels large and small, green and spotted, had come all the way out into the open and were chasing us.

Impossible. Morays *never* left the safety of their holes.

Oh, really?

We knew there was no point trying to flee. The morays could catch us in a wink. And they did. And once they had us at their mercy, they . . . did nothing. They chased us, caught up with us, and passed us by.

It was frightening and—once we knew they didn't intend to bite us—fascinating. None of us had ever seen anything like it before, and I haven't since.

KILLER WHALES (ORCAS)

If there's an animal in the sea that great white sharks are afraid of, it's the killer whale. Among meat eaters, it is *the* apex predator in the ocean. (Sperm whales, which are much bigger, are—technically—meat eaters, too, but their diet consists mostly of squid.) Though killer whales are officially members of the dolphin family, they make most dolphins seem like house pets. Males can grow to thirty feet long and weigh several tons.

Killer whales do eat mammals, and they have attacked and sunk boats. But there is *not one* recorded instance of an orca in the wild attacking a human being. There are, though, a couple of instances of captive killer whales turning on and wounding their trainers.

I was aware of all the facts and statistics when, in the 1980s, I was asked to go scuba diving in the wild with killer whales. But the facts were cold comfort. I didn't know anybody who had ever gone into the water with wild killer whales on purpose, so there was no one to call for advice. I thought that perhaps the reason nobody had ever been attacked was that nobody had ever been in the water with one. Maybe I'd be the test case, the first one, the late, lucky loser.

The first protective measure I took was to have a wet suit custom-made. It was puke green with yellow piping on the arms and legs and a broad yellow stripe across the chest. I wanted to broadcast to any and all killer whales, *I am not a seal!* I considered having the actual words stenciled within the yellow stripe. But even I knew that, smart as they are, killer whales can't read.

Killer whales exist in all the oceans of the world, in warm water and cold. According to Richard Ellis, they're the most widely distributed of all cetaceans (dolphins and whales). Their common name comes from the documented fact that they kill other whales. Pods of killer whales will gang up on one of the great whales—a blue whale, say—and kill it and eat it.

I was to dive with them in the cold Canadian waters of the Johnstone Strait, off Vancouver Island. Several pods that lived there were being studied by scientists. Specifically, there was a stony beach where killer whales were known to come to rub themselves on the round rocks, called rubbing rocks. The whales do it either to rid themselves of minute parasites or, more likely, just for the fun of it. The plan was for Stan Waterman and me to lie on the rocky bottom, using oxygen re-breathers so as not to generate bubbles (whales hear bubbles, know that they mean people, and stay away). We were supposed to wait for the whales to arrive. Then, with ABC's primitive videocamera hardwired to a monitor on the beach, we would capture images of them rubbing. (This has been done a thousand times since, but up till then it had never been done.)

I met my first killer whale before I even got wet. A local scientist and I were traveling across the Johnstone Strait in a rubber boat when we came upon a pod of orcas cruising easily in open water. We stopped the engine and drifted. Within five minutes the whales surrounded us, clicking and tweeping and chattering among themselves. There was a big male—easily identifiable by his five- or six-foot-high dorsal fin—along with a couple of females and a few youngsters.

Without warning, one of the youngsters—twelve or

thirteen feet long and as big around as a barrel—surged out of the water. It plopped its head on the side of the rubber boat. It opened its mouth, displaying its pink tongue and its huge conical teeth.

Shocked, I flinched and backed away.

"He wants you to scratch his tongue," the scientist said.

"Right," I replied, thinking that at this moment jokes were in rather bad taste.

"I'm serious. Go ahead."

I stared at him and at the whale, which was waiting patiently, mouth open, emitting an occasional click or cheep. Then I decided that a one-armed writer could still be a writer. So I very gingerly touched the whale's tongue and gave it a scratch.

"All the way back," the scientist said. "Right at the base. And really scratch it."

I took a deep breath and plunged my arm into the whale's mouth up to my shoulder. With my hand out of sight in the back of the dark cavern, I scratched for all I was worth.

The whale purred. I'm not kidding—it *purred,* just like a happy cat. And I—from the pit of my stomach to the back of my neck, where the hairs stood on end and tingled—felt overwhelmed. It was as if I was communicating not only with this young whale but also with nature itself. I'd never experienced anything like it.

I looked at the scientist and grinned, and he grinned back. I scratched some more; the whale purred some more. I would've kept scratching all day. But after a while the scientist said, "That'll do," and I withdrew my arm. The whale closed its mouth and slid gently back into the sea.

The rest of our experiment with the killer whales of the Johnstone Strait was pretty uneventful. The water was wickedly cold, so we began by using dry suits. Dry suits, as the name implies, are intended to keep the diver dry and warm instead of, as in the case of a wet suit, wet and clammy. But I have never gotten the hang of maneuvering inside what amounts to a gigantic space suit. I didn't know how to adjust my buoyancy. Air pockets formed and shifted, so I hung crookedly, then shot to the surface upside down and backward. I gave up warmth in favor of balance and switched back to my wet suit. It allowed me ten or fifteen minutes of feeling in my hands and feet and approximately half an hour of consciousness.

The water over the rubbing rocks was only five or six feet deep but very murky (visibility between five and ten feet). Stan and I lay on the bottom and waited for a pod of whales to come along for a rub.

We heard them long before we saw them. The clicks, whistles, and tweeps, I learned later, were the whales discussing us. Their supersensitive sonar picked us up from half a mile away, but they couldn't decide what we were. They knew we were alive and not fish, warm-blooded but not seals or sea lions. We gave off no bubbles. Evidently, we were worth investigating, for the whales continued toward us. Their conversation grew louder and more excited. (Stan and I were each convinced that the whales' discussion was about which of them would have the privilege of deciding which of us to eat first.)

The whale sounds grew louder and louder as they came closer and closer. Still we could see nothing but thick gray murk.

Suddenly, like a flash-cut in a movie, the frame of our vision was filled with an enormous black-and-white head rushing at us. The jaws were open; each cone of sharp white ivory shone like a blade.

And then the whale actually *saw* us. It recognized us for what we were, and immediately—impossibly quickly— veered away. It let out a loud, long *blaaat,* the whale equivalent of booing. I thought its meaning was vividly clear: disgust and dismay at being fooled by two dumb, clumsy, and decidedly inferior beings.

The immense body vanished, and no other whales appeared. As the pod pulled away from us, the tone of their discussion returned to a level of calm, dull conversation.

POISONOUS ANIMALS

The oceans are full of creatures that depend on poison as a weapon of defense or offense. They range from anemones to corals to jellyfish, cone shells, bony fish, and air-breathing snakes.

Swimmers, in general, don't have to worry about any but the jellyfish. But there are many kinds of jellyfish, some far more poisonous than others. It makes sense for a swimmer to seek the advice of locals before galloping willy-nilly into the water.

In Australia, for example, there are box jellyfish, called sea wasps. Their poison can, and occasionally does, kill a human being. At certain times of the year some beaches along Australia's northeast coast are closed to swimmers and surfers because of the seasonal invasion of sea wasps.

One of the most common dangerous jellyfish in the Atlantic is the Portuguese man-of-war. Its tentacles deliver a toxin that, while not usually fatal, causes excruciating pain and can be debilitating. The best thing that can be said about men-of-war is that you can see them coming. They are wind-and-current-driven jellies with "sails" like purple balloons that extend several inches above the surface. Even though they are visible, it's best to give them a wide berth. Their stinging tentacles can stretch as much as a hundred feet below and, depending on the current, to the side.

There are dozens of other stinging jellyfish that are more nuisance than menace. Almost all of them (including the sea wasps and the men-of-war) share a fascinating technology of attack. Their tentacles shoot microscopic harpoons into their victims, and the harpoons inject powerful nerve poisons.

Humans are never any jellyfish's intended victim. A small

fish stung to death by, say, a man-of-war is drawn up under the body and eaten with what Ellis calls "feeding polyps."

There are almost as many proposed remedies for jellyfish stings as there are kinds of jellyfish—vinegar, urine, meat tenderizer, alcohol, seawater, and shampoo, to name a few. Many of them work, more or less. It depends on the kind of jellyfish that has stung you, the amount of tentacle matter that has made contact with your skin, and how sensitive you are to the particular poison that has been injected. A woman I know swam face-on into one of the notorious "red jellies" that infest the Northeast every August. She had to be hospitalized for a couple of days. At the same time a cousin of hers dove through a crowd of the same jellies and was stung all over her torso. All she felt was an annoying tingling sensation.

Many poisonous fish are of the family *Scorpaenidae*. This includes the scorpion fish, the lionfish, and the stonefish. They are found in tropical waters and normally live near, on, or in the bottom. That's a blessing for swimmers and snorkelers because many of the family members are deadly. They have highly venomous spines on their backs, which are used entirely defensively, so no one need worry about being attacked by one. Stepping on one, however, is another concern altogether. They make wading around reefs a perilous pastime.

Scuba divers worry about the *Scorpaenidae* for yet another reason. Underwater and within the chaos of color that is a tropical reef, they're almost invisible. Stonefish, which according to Ellis are the deadliest fish in the world, can look *exactly* like a rock covered with marine growth. They lie half hidden in the sand and wait for potential prey to come by. A wader who steps on one or a diver who reaches out to steady herself on this apparent rock may be stabbed by dorsal spines fed by venom glands. Untreated, an adult human can die in less than two hours.

Lionfish look like gaudy Christmas-tree ornaments. They are bold and armed with long venomous dorsal spines. They don't bother to hide, not in sand or reef, and they rarely retreat at the approach of a human. Instead, they'll seem to aim their spines your way, as if daring you to take your best shot. To me, the prime danger of a lionfish lies in its ability to disappear from view against the background of a particularly spectacular reef. Several times I've blundered up to and among lionfish without seeing them. Only good fortune has protected me from bumping or putting a hand on one.

I've had very little close contact with poisonous sea snakes, most of which live in the Indo-Pacific. Almost all of them want nothing whatever to do with human beings. There are several species, and most are at least as venomous as the Indian cobra. But their fangs are very short and their temperaments usually placid. During breeding season, however, some species can become aggressive. A couple of friends of mine have been surprised by snakes heading for the surface to breathe that suddenly reversed course, charged, and bit them. My friends' quarter-inch-thick wet suits prevented the snakes' fangs from reaching their skin, or at least slowed the bite enough to give my friends time to grab the snakes and fling them away before fang touched flesh.

BARRACUDAS

If ever there was a fish that's gotten a bad rap solely for being bad-looking, it's the barracuda. A barracuda can grow to be up to six feet long and is slender, tough, and fast as lightning. It is armed with a prognathous lower jaw (it extends forward beyond the upper one) studded with dozens of jagged, needle-sharp teeth designed to tear prey to shreds. A barracuda looks mean, menacing, and deadly. (I speak here specifically of the great barracuda, the largest of the more than twenty species that roam the tropical waters of the world.)

The image is a phony. The great barracuda is capable, no question, of causing serious bodily harm to any of us. But it has no inclination to do so. It feeds on fish, and its speed and weaponry are so formidable that it has little difficulty catching and killing whatever it wants.

There have been very, very few cases of barracudas biting people. All those I've heard of were almost certainly accidents of misidentification. A swimmer wears a shiny watch, ring, or buckle into the surf, where visibility is poor, and a barracuda mistakes a flash of reflected light for the shimmer of fish scales. It bites, instantly recognizes its error, and vanishes. Sometimes the bite is so fast and efficient that the person doesn't know he's been bitten.

Divers are used to seeing barracudas appear from nowhere. These fish hang around and gaze with fixed eye at whatever's going on, then disappear with the same impossible speed. Sometimes they come very close and hover, motionless, watching. Usually, they establish and somehow maintain a precise distance from the divers, advancing and retreating without appearing to flutter a single fin.

I have never heard of a barracuda seeing a human being, watching, studying, and evaluating him, and then turning on him and biting him. Never.

Which was no comfort at all when one day I took Wendy and then-twelve-year-old Clayton drift diving off Palm Beach, Florida.

Drift diving is diving in—and with—a strong current. It is done in circumstances where swimming against the current is difficult, dangerous, or downright impossible. Divers leave the boat in one location and drift along with the current. They hold a line tied to an inflated ball that bobs on the surface so the captain of the boat can keep track of them. Then the boat picks them up far down-current when the dive is done.

Palm Beach is perfect for drift diving because one of the

world's great currents, the Gulf Stream, touches the shore right there. The Gulf Stream then sweeps north and eventually northeast, warming the Atlantic waters all the way from Bermuda to Newfoundland and points east. Dive boats can deposit divers only a couple of hundred yards offshore. They are instantly seized by the warm, four-knot current and carried along with the entire movable feast that inhabits the Gulf Stream.

Four of us jumped into the choppy water—we three and a dive master, who held the line tied to the floating ball. We quickly sank to the calm and quiet thirty or forty feet down. The water was so rich in nutrients that it was cloudy. Visibility was terrible, and Wendy and I made sure to keep our eyes on both Clayton and the dive master.

There wasn't much to see, however, and Clayton soon became impatient. We weren't roaring along fast enough for him, so he sped up by kicking with the current.

Within thirty seconds he had vanished into the gloom.

Though Wendy and I were both concerned, we weren't particularly worried. He couldn't stray too far, and he could only stray in one direction because he couldn't possibly swim against the current.

Then there he was, suddenly, chugging directly at us. He was swimming against the current, kicking as fast as his fins would flutter and breast-stroking with his arms. He stared at us through the faceplate of his mask, his eyes wide with fear. He was actually making headway, and when he reached us, he kept swimming until he was behind me. Then he stopped struggling, grabbed me, and climbed aboard my back.

I looked at Wendy, who was looking at Clayton. Clayton was pointing somewhere ahead. He was exhausted, and he breathed so fast that bubbles exploded from his regulator in a constant stream.

We looked, following his finger, but saw nothing. I was beginning to assume that Clayton had come up behind and perhaps startled a shark that had turned toward him, scaring him out of his wits. Then I saw Wendy pointing and then the dive master pointing. There, a few yards ahead and below, was what looked like a big school of big sharks. They were just cruising along in the current, as if waiting for food to be carried to them.

But they weren't sharks. As we drifted closer and closer, they slowly rose to meet us until we were actually drifting *among* them. I saw that they were barracudas, and not merely great barracudas, for the word *great* doesn't do them justice. They were super-, mega-, Moby Dick barracudas, barracudas on steroids.

I couldn't believe it. Even allowing for the fact that, underwater, everything looks a third again as big as it really is, these monsters couldn't be real. They looked at *least* twelve feet long, which meant that they were really nine feet long.

Nine-foot barracudas! They were two feet high and one foot thick, and each one's mouth looked like a Swiss army knife open for display. Their eyes stared at us with the blank serenity of the invulnerable.

As we continued to drift together, these great creatures paid us no attention whatsoever. In fact, they moved aside to avoid contact with us, and I could finally see them in proper perspective.

There were probably a dozen of them—it was hard to tell, for they drifted in and out of sight. Each one was probably five or six feet long and very high and very thick. As I gazed at each silver giant, I now saw, instead of ugliness, the beauty of perfection. For in their world these creatures were supreme. They went where they wanted, ate what they chose, and feared no living thing.

When at last we surfaced and were back on the boat, Clayton said, "I think I'd like to be a barracuda."

RAYS

The oceans are full of rays of all kinds, colors, shapes, and sizes. All are "cousins" of the sharks, in that they're technically elasmobranchs. That means that their bodies are structured not with bones but with cartilage. They include everything from sawfishes to guitarfishes to manta rays, eagle rays, and stingrays. Except for the most bizarre of accidental circumstances, they're harmless to humans.

But what about stingrays? I hear you yowling. *They have stingers, don't they? They can sting you, can't they?*

Yes, they can, if you step on them. But so can bees. And a bald eagle can claw your eyes out, and a German shepherd can rip your throat out, and a raccoon can give you rabies. But the chances are, they won't.

Anyone who needs convincing of the gentleness of stingrays need travel no farther than the Cayman Islands. Local dive groups there have established a dive site called Stingray City in the sand flats off Grand Cayman. Stingrays gather there in numbers far too large to count, and they wait patiently for the boats that arrive daily with divers and food. The rays swim up to you, under your arms, between your legs, and around your head. They envelop you with wings as soft as satin. They feed from your hand, and if you have nothing for them, they move on to someone else. (Even stingrays can make mistakes, however. A few years ago, one mistook my son-in-law's wrist for a tender morsel and actually bit him. The hard cartilaginous plates in the ray's mouth caused a nasty bruise but didn't break the skin.)

It's very tempting to anthropomorphize stingrays. Not only do they behave calmly and comfortably around humans, but when seen from underneath, they can even look humanoid, if you'll let your imagination ramble a bit. The nostrils look like eyes, the mouth is a mouth, and the point of the head can become a nose, and . . . well, you have to be there.

Twenty years ago I had an experience with a ray that changed my life. Literally. I hurried home and wrote a book about it—*The Girl of the Sea of Cortez*. It altered forever my perception of animals, people, the sea, and the interconnectedness of everything on earth.

I was in the Sea of Cortez, doing an *American Sportsman* segment on hammerhead sharks. For reasons no one has ever been able to explain, hammerheads gather there periodically in huge, peaceful schools of hundreds, perhaps thousands, at a time. The gatherings seem to have nothing to do with either breeding or feeding. The hammerheads are simply there, in crowds so thick that seen from below, they block the sun.

The underwater cameramen on the shoot were old friends, Stan Waterman and Howard Hall. Howard's wife, Michele, who's now a producer, director, and partner in Howard's film company, was along as both nurse and still photographer.

One afternoon we returned to our chartered boat, the *Don Jose,* full of macho tales of death-defying diving among the sea monsters. We were interrupted by a very excited Michele, who directed us to look beneath the boat.

There, basking in the boat's cool shadow, was the largest manta ray any of us had ever seen. (We'd soon learn that it measured eighteen feet from wingtip to wingtip. At the moment, all we knew was that it looked as big as an F-16.) A manta has fins near its head that unfurl during feeding and become supple sweeps to gather food into its immense mouth. Now they were rolled up tightly, and they looked exactly like horns—thus, the manta's age-old traditional name, devilfish.

For centuries the manta was one of the most terrifying animals in the sea. It is huge, horned, and winged, with a mouth big enough to swallow a person whole. It also has a habit of leaping clear out of the water, turning somersaults, and slamming down upon the surface of the sea. Obviously it's daring any foolish sailor to fall overboard into its ghastly grasp. Equally obviously, such hideous monsters deserved no fate better than death. Spearing mantas used to be a popular sport among the few, the bold, and the brave.

In fact, mantas are harmless. They eat only plankton and other microscopic sea life. They breach (soar out of the water) for reasons no one knows for certain. They probably do it to rid themselves of parasites but possibly, as I prefer to believe, do it just for the fun of it. Usually, they avoid people, swimming—*flying* seems more accurate—slowly away from approaching divers.

Sometimes, however, they seem to seek the company of people, like the manta that now rested peacefully beneath our boat. Before any of us could ask, Michele told us how she had discovered the magnificent creature.

The air temperature was well above a hundred degrees Fahrenheit. The *Don Jose* was not air-conditioned. To keep bearably cool, Michele went overboard frequently. On one of her plunges she had seen the enormous ray hovering motionless beneath the boat. She swam toward it. It didn't move. As she drew near, she saw that the animal was injured. Where one wing joined the body there was a tear in the flesh, and the wound was full of rope. Michele supposed that the manta had swum blindly into one of the countless nets set by fishermen all over the Sea of Cortez. In struggling to free itself, which it had accomplished not with teeth (they have none) but with sheer strength, it had torn its wing and carried pieces of the broken net away with it.

Michele kept expecting the manta to ease away from her as she approached. But by now she was almost on top of it and still it hadn't moved. She was, however, out of breath. She decided to return to the boat and put on scuba gear.

The manta was still there when she returned. This time she was emitting noisy streams of bubbles, and she knew that the manta would probably flee from them.

It didn't.

Slowly, she let herself fall gently down until she was sitting on the manta's back.

Still it didn't move.

Michele reached forward and, very gingerly, pulled strand after strand of thick rope netting out of the ragged wound. She had no idea how—or even if—rays experience pain. But if they did, she thought, this *had* to hurt.

The manta lay perfectly still.

When all the rope was gone, Michele carefully packed the shreds of torn flesh together and pressed them into the cavity in the wing. She covered the wound with her hands.

Now the manta came to life. Very slowly it raised its wings and brought them down again. Very slowly the great body began to move forward, not with enough speed to throw Michele off its back but with an easy, casual pace that let her ride comfortably along. To steady herself Michele put one hand on the manta's six-foot-wide upper lip. Off they went, with Michele's heart pounding in her chest, happiness filling her heart, amazement and delight flooding her mind.

The boat was anchored on a sea mount, an underwater mountain whose peak extended to within a hundred feet of the surface. With unimaginable grace the manta took Michele on a flying tour of the entire mountaintop. Down it flew to the edge of darkness, then up again to the surface light.

Michele didn't know how long the ride lasted—fifteen minutes, maybe half an hour. But eventually the manta returned to its station in the shadow of the boat and stopped. Michele let go and came to the surface. She was thrilled beyond words, but she thought we would never believe her. Surely by the time we came back, the manta would have long since returned to its home range, wherever that might be.

But it hadn't. It was still there, still resting in the cool, still apparently—impossibly!—willing to have more contact with humans.

We decided to try to capture the manta on film. We knew we couldn't duplicate Michele's experience. But even if we could get some shots of the great ray flying away with a human being in the same frame to give a sense of its size, we'd have some very special film.

Howard and Stan filmed the ray itself from every possible angle. Then they signaled for me to descend, as Michele had, and attempt to land gently on the manta's back. I had done my best to neutralize my buoyancy so that, once submerged, my 180 pounds would weigh nothing. Now I used my hands like little fins to guide me down upon the animal as lightly as a butterfly.

As soon as the manta felt my presence on its back, it started forward. It flew very slowly at first, but soon its wings fell into a long, graceful sweep. It was flying so fast that I—in order to stay aboard—had to grip its upper lip with one hand and a wing with the other and lie flat against its back. My mask was mashed against my face, we were going so fast. My hair was plastered back so hard that on film I look bald.

I felt like a fighter pilot—no, not a pilot, for I had no control over this craft. It was more like being a passenger in a fighter plane. Down we flew, and banked around the sea mount, and soared again. We passed turtles that didn't give us a passing glance and hammerheads that (I swear) did a double take as they saw us go by.

The world grew dark, and for a moment I was afraid. I knew we had gone very deep, but I had no way of knowing exactly how deep because I couldn't let go with one hand to reach for my depth gauge. *If we're too deep,* I worried, *I'll run out of air, or get the bends on surfacing, or—*

Just then, as if to reassure me, the manta returned to the world of light. It rushed for the surface, gaining speed with every thrust of its mighty wings. I had the sudden, terrifying conviction that it was going to burst through the surface and take to the air—and me with it. When we slammed down again on the water I would be reduced to pudding. But long before it reached the surface, the manta swerved away and began to cruise twenty or thirty feet below the boat.

Finally, it slowed, then silently stopped directly in the shadow of the boat. I let go and made my way to the surface.

Like Michele, I didn't know how long my journey had lasted, and there was no way to find out. My air tank was almost empty. Stan and Howard had each run through a full load of film, which meant that I had been underwater on that magical ride for at least twenty minutes. But how deep, and for how long, at what depth? The only way I would know how much nitrogen—the villain that brings on bends—was left in my system was to wait. If I came down with the agony of the bends, in my joints or my guts, I'd know I had gone too deep for too long. If I didn't, I'd know I hadn't. Simple as that.

The manta, meanwhile, stayed beneath the boat. Over the next three days, every member of the crew had a chance to swim with or ride on the manta. Always, without exception, the wonderful ray returned its passengers to the same exact spot beneath the boat.

As soon as I returned home, I began to write. A story had been born, entire, in my head. I wrote it at record speed (for me) and with thoughts, feelings, and perceptions I didn't know I had.

It was published as the novel *The Girl of the Sea of Cortez.* Though it's now out of print, I'm delighted that readers are still discovering it, for it is my favorite of all my books about the sea.

Though the book still clings to life, I'm sorry to report that the magical manta rays of the Sea of Cortez do not. Too many fishermen lost too many nets to the mantas. So they hunted them down until there were none left.

SQUID—GIANT AND OTHERWISE

Of all the creatures that have ever lived in the sea, none has generated more groundless fears and fabulous fantasies than the giant squid. Jules Verne had a giant squid attack the submarine *Nautilus* in *20,000 Leagues Under the Sea.* I wrote a novel about a giant squid, titled *Beast,* which NBC made into a miniseries. And Richard Ellis, who knows more than I ever will about giant squid, published a fine nonfiction book called *The Search for the Giant Squid.*

Ellis's title is exactly on target. Almost the entire history of man's relationship with this formidable animal has been a search, and a fruitless one at that. One of the main reasons— if not *the* main reason—for our endless fascination with this monster of monsters is that so little is known about it. And the reason for *that* is that despite twenty-first-century technology and the best efforts of battalions of scientists and adventurers, no one has ever seen a giant squid alive in the ocean. What fragments are known have been gathered from studies of specimens either dead or dying in the nets that have trapped them.

Here is a summary of what's known about giant squid. (I've combined facts from Ellis's encyclopedia and my own experiences, conversations, and reading.)

Their scientific name is *Architeuthis*, which translates from the Greek (roughly) as "first among squid." Not first in line but first in importance, as in "squid of all squid" or, in today's language, "Man, you de *squiiiid.*" There are more than a dozen different species of *Architeuthis*. Most are named for the place their corpses were found. But amateurs like me bundle them all together with the single name *Architeuthis dux:* king of kings of squid. Sort of.

They are the largest of the more than seven hundred kinds of squid that live in the world's oceans. The biggest one accepted by science was a dead animal found decades ago washed up on a New Zealand shore. It was complete, and was measured at fifty-seven feet long, from its tail to the tip of its two whips, or feeding tentacles. (Unlike octopuses, squid have ten arms, eight short ones plus the two whips.)

The biggest one accepted by me was seventy-three feet long. By the time it washed up on a beach in eastern Canada, some of its arms had been eaten away, so it could not be accurately measured. But scientists studying the remains decided that the animal would have been seventy-three feet long.

I'm even prepared to believe that somewhere in the deep ocean there lives a giant squid more than a hundred feet long. While I was doing research for *Beast* more than a decade ago, I spoke by phone with one of the world's two great teuthologists (squid scientists). He was ill then and would soon die. Though he was helpful, he insisted that I not attribute anything he said directly to him, for he didn't want to risk his reputation. He told me that his lifetime of study had convinced him that the existence of a *150-foot* giant squid was not only possible but probable.

Imagine a squid half the length of a football field . . . a squid that, standing on end, would reach fifteen stories into the air . . . a squid longer than three locomotives . . . a squid . . . well, you get the idea.

Giant squid seem to inhabit the oceans' midwater range, between 1,800 and 3,500 feet. That, at least, is where most of the specimens caught recently in fishing nets have been found. There is practically no light at those depths except for what is generated by creatures that are bioluminescent—that is, creatures who give off their own light (like many squid). Giant squid have enormous eyes (the largest in the animal kingdom) that can reach a diameter of fifteen inches. Such huge eyes can gather in every available atom of light.

Throughout history (all the way back to Homer's *Odyssey*) there have been stories of giant squid attacking and sinking ships. Many of these tales have been supported by witnesses and newspaper accounts, but none has been completely authenticated. Countless stories exist of monster squid assaulting fishermen and plucking unlucky shipwreck survivors from lifeboats. None of those stories would stand up in court, either. But I'm convinced that several, though perhaps wildly exaggerated, spring from seeds of truth. There are simply too many accounts by too many rational people for them *all* to be fantasies or hallucinations.

Certainly, giant squid are capable of wreaking havoc on small boats and all humans. A giant squid does not have claws within each sucker on its tentacles—claws that are present in many smaller, more aggressive species of squid. But its suckers *do* have rings of hard, sharp "teeth" made of chitin (the same stuff some mollusk shells are made of). These "teeth" gnaw into prey and drag it toward the animal's big, sharp beak. The beak, in turn, slashes the prey to pieces and feeds it to the squid's studded tongue, which forces the flesh down into the gut.

A lovely way to go, no?

Among the many things *not* known about giant squid are how big they can grow, how fast they grow, and how long they live. We don't know exactly what they feed on (it *is* known that sperm whales feed on *them*). We don't know where they hang out, whether or not they are aggressive, whether or not they are as immensely powerful as legend insists, or why, every year, all over the world, a great many giant squid just seem to die. Because their flesh is loaded with ammonium ions, which are lighter than water, their bodies float rather than sink. Some are eaten by sharks and other fish, but some float all the way to shore more or less intact.

My fascination with giant squid began in the late 1970s, when Teddy Tucker and I decided to try to catch one off Bermuda. Giant-squid bodies—and pieces of bodies—were found floating on the surface there quite often. We went out at night and from the stern of his boat lowered two three-thousand-foot lengths of cable woven of forty-eight strands of stainless steel. Each cable carried clusters of baited hooks of varying sizes, plus Cyalume chemical lights. We hoped the lights would attract the squid's attention.

We had visions of grotesque monsters in the gloomy deep, throbbing with the colors of excitement (all squid can change color at split-second speeds) as they attacked our baits. We imagined titanic struggles as the cables thrummed with strain and spat droplets of water from each stressed strand. We imagined the stern of the boat being pulled down, down, until—perhaps—Teddy would decide that the only way to save our lives would be to sever the cables with the axe he had stowed nearby.

We waited all night, bouncing around in rough seas, and got no nibbles on either cable. At dawn, filled with disappointment, we began to haul in the cables on giant spools.

They came in easily. Too easily, in fact. *Strange*.

The five-hundred-foot marker passed, then the thousand-foot. With every turn of the spool the cable seemed lighter, much lighter, weirdly light. The fifteen-hundred-foot marker passed, and now the cables felt *too* light. Definitely.

Over the stern the cables popped. The lights were gone, the baits were gone, the hooks were gone. The final thousand feet of cable were gone.

The cables had been severed. They hadn't popped from weight or stress; the strands were all still tightly wrapped. They had been cut. Bitten off.

Gloom gave way to excitement. What could have done this? Not a shark. No gigantic fish had swallowed the baited hooks and tried to run with them. We would have felt it; the boat would have moved. And no shark tooth was hard enough to cut through an eighth of an inch of stainless steel.

We couldn't have foul-hooked a whale. Sure, the weight of a whale would have been enough to break the cable. But the cable ends would be splayed, the strands all askew.

Whatever had bitten through our cables, we decided, had a beak as hard as Kevlar, a material used in bulletproof vests, among other things. (How, you ask, could we make that leap of logic? Easy: we wanted to.) And what had such a beak?

Why, nothing—nothing, that is, except a giant squid.

Clearly, this was an animal worth pursuing.

We tried the next year, and the next. We've tried, in fact,

every year since then. Always we've been teased; never have we been successful.

We've hung cameras down to two and three thousand feet and focused them on baited hooks. We've seen creatures bizarre and wonderful, including vicious little squid that savaged our bait till nothing was left but scales. We've seen curious, unknown sharks that live only in that particular part of the deep. But we've never seen a sign of *Architeuthis*.

One day we set a baited line half a mile down and buoyed it with three rubber balls, each designed to float five hundred pounds. We left the line for a couple of hours while we went to set others. When we returned, the balls were gone.

For fifteen or twenty minutes we searched back and forth. There was no question that we were in the right place. Teddy has an uncanny ability to locate himself in the open ocean, especially off Bermuda, where he can pinpoint his position using landmarks.

The balls were gone. Simple as that.

Just as we were about to abandon them—yet another mystery never to be solved—there was a roaring, whooshing sound off the port side of Teddy's boat. One by one—*Pow! Pow! Pow!*—the three balls burst through the surface, still connected together. They bobbed placidly on the calm sea, as if they'd never been gone at all.

When we pulled in the half mile of line, all the hooks were gone, as were all the baits. Once again, the strands of the rope were still tightly bound. Something had pulled and pulled and pulled, with a force great enough to sink three quarters of a ton, and then bitten through the rope.

In the early 1990s, when I was host of an ESPN series of shows called *Expedition Earth,* we spent nearly three years putting together an hour on giant squid. We knew that we had next to no chance of being able to film one in the wild. So we filmed some of the animals closely associated with *Architeuthis.*

We traveled again to Canada, this time to dive—in January, no less, and in falling snow—with the squid's fabulous cousin, the giant octopus. Giant octopuses have been documented to grow as large as sixteen feet in diameter. They are shy, reclusive, and, when they can be coaxed out of their dens, fascinating to watch. As they scurry across the sea floor, they change color and pattern to camouflage themselves to match the bottom they're on or over.

We swam with Caribbean sperm whales in the deep waters around Dominica and Martinique. We were hoping—against all odds—to catch some interaction between whale and squid. The only squid I saw, however, were ex-squid, former squid, squid that were no more. As I snorkeled beside a fifty-foot-long adult sperm whale, it dove down suddenly. As a parting gift it left me enveloped in a thick red cloud of eaten, digested, and excreted giant squid.

We acquired old woodcut prints of beached giant squid and amateur video footage of giant squid killed in fishing nets. Howard Hall shot some extraordinary footage of a hundred-pound Humboldt squid ripping apart a big tuna being hand-fed to it. Humboldt squid are considered to be more dangerous to man than any shark. (One of Howard's other colleagues was later attacked by three Humboldt squid and was lucky to escape with his life.)

In the end we put together a good hour-long show that was, I believe, informative and entertaining. But we never succeeded in finding a single giant squid.

Over the past decade, more and more dead and dying giant squid have been caught by net fishermen, particularly in the waters off New Zealand. The reason is not a sudden population increase in giant squid. The reason is that relatively recent technological advances have given deep-sea trawlers access to fish in water two thousand to five thousand feet deep. There the squid spend a good deal of their time feeding on, among other things, a species of fish called orange roughy.

Orange roughies are amazing fish, only about a foot long, that can live for more than a century. Ellis says that "there are documented records of individuals that have reached 150." They don't mature until they're about thirty years old. Because they tend to gather in tight schools, they're easy prey for deep trawlers. A five-minute trawl, according to Ellis, "can fill a trawl net with ten to fifty tons of fish."

Consequently, orange roughies are being wiped out at an alarming rate. The fishery is only twenty-six years old, and already catches have declined drastically. Some scientists believe that orange roughies may eventually set a record for the speed with which any species (of anything) has gone from initial discovery to commercial extinction.

Meanwhile, though, the presence of giant squid among the orange-roughy populations has lured legions of passionate teuthophiles (squid lovers). Scientists, writers, divers, and filmmakers have gone out on multimillion-dollar expeditions to find giant squid by using submersibles, fifty-thousand-dollar-a-day ships, and the highest of high-tech locating gear.

None has ever seen a giant squid, let alone caught one or filmed a live one swimming in the sea. And, I confess, I'm glad.

Architeuthis is one of the few true mysteries left on earth. It is an animal of mythic stature that we know exists but that we cannot find. It is a real creature that is at the same time an ancient, enduring legend. It is a spur to scientific quest and an inspiration to our imagination.

It is the last dragon. We need our dragons, for they help our fancies soar beyond the boundaries of reality.

I hope the giant squid successfully eludes us for years to come.

14

Even More Creatures to Avoid . . . and Respect

Among the immense citizenry of the sea there are many other living things that appear to be inert, passive, and harmless—or alive and friendly. But these creatures can be dangerous if you are inexperienced, careless, or unlucky.

Many **corals** are poisonous to the touch. They possess stinging cells that are used both for self-defense and to paralyze prey. The most common of the poisonous corals—at least as far as swimmers, snorkelers, and divers are concerned—is fire coral. Fire coral looks like mustard that has been painted onto parts of a reef. Slick, motionless, and harmless-looking, fire coral can deliver a thoroughly nasty sting to an exploring hand.

Sea anemones are poisonous, too. Their beautiful, waving tentacles seem harmless because colorful little fish swim all around them with no ill effects. In fact, each tentacle can fire toxic harpoons into anything that touches them. The colorful little fish (usually clownfish) are coated with a mucus that makes them immune to the anemone's poison. The relationship is pure symbiosis. The anemone protects the clownfish from other predators. In return, the clownfish removes food particles and other debris from the anemone, keeping it clean and healthy.

Several species of **mantis shrimp** can grow to be more than a foot long. These shrimp live in the North Atlantic, the Mediterranean, and the seas around Australia, where they're known as killer prawns. Each has a pair of limbs that fold like the forearms of a praying mantis (hence the name). The limbs unfold like a jackknife, at what seems like the speed of light. The blades are so strong and sharp that they can amputate a human finger with a single stroke. Mantis shrimp are fearless and aggressive. I know several underwater photographers who are seriously afraid of them. When a photographer is concentrating on getting a shot of a tiny creature hiding in a reef, he isn't thinking about what might be burrowed in the sand beside him, ready to pounce and slash his flesh to ribbons.

Spiny sea urchins, black, bristly balls that live on the sea bottom, are harmless—until you happen to step on or bump into one. Then one or more of the hundreds of spines spear you and break off in your flesh. Some species have poisonous spines and some don't, but *any* urchin spine is amazingly painful. They are difficult to get out (they keep breaking apart into smaller and smaller pieces) and can cause infection.

Some oceangoing critters are obviously dangerous and

to be avoided at all costs. **Saltwater crocodiles** leap quickly to mind. Years ago I worked with a researcher from the National Geographic Society to put together a list of the ten most dangerous animals in the world. We found it impossible not to include saltwater crocodiles.

They live all over the western Pacific, in freshwater rivers and brackish swamps as well as in the sea. They eat just about anything they can catch, and they stalk and catch almost anything. They will go after birds, monkeys, turtles, fish, crabs, buffaloes, and—as documented many times—human beings. They're known to grow to be at least twenty-three feet long (In *Encyclopedia of the Sea,* Richard Ellis says they're the largest of all the living reptiles). They regularly swim hundreds of miles out into the open ocean.

A friend of mine was once thinking about a trip around the Pacific in a collapsible kayak. One part of his journey would take him across the Torres Strait, which separates northern Australia from New Guinea. He asked me about the chances of his encountering aggressive sharks. I told him I wouldn't be half so afraid of sharks as of the "salties." These crocodiles have been known to attack and destroy boats much more substantial than collapsible kayaks.

Other sea creatures have completely surprised me when, over the years, I've discovered they can be dangerous. But in every case I've come to realize that it's the human that has gotten in harm's way, not the animal that's suddenly turned mean.

I'm speaking here specifically of **groupers, bluefish,** and, believe it or not, certain species of **dolphins**.

The one dicey moment I've witnessed with a grouper happened in Turks and Caicos Islands, a small group of islands south of the Bahamas. A woman in our crew had decided to go for a swim during the heat of the day. She dove off the boat without giving a thought to the fact that she was in a very active phase of her menstrual cycle.

She had surfaced from her dive and wiped her hair back from her face when she felt something bump her, very hard, in the thigh, and then bite her.

She shouted and lashed out with her feet, trying to back away. She wasn't wearing a mask or fins, so she couldn't see what had bitten her. She couldn't escape quickly, either. It pursued her, bit her again, and kept coming. Again she shouted.

Those of us on board heard her shout, ran to the side, and looked overboard. Through the clear water we could see everything. A small (eight- or ten-pound) Nassau grouper had, we assumed, scented blood in the water and, following its instinct, attacked the source. It didn't matter that the animal it was attacking was more than ten times its size. That animal was bleeding, and blood meant injury, weakness, and vulnerability.

It took us a few seconds to realize that what we were watching was not funny. Then two of us jumped overboard, one right behind the swimmer, one right on top of the grouper.

The grouper was startled to find that the sky had fallen on its head, and shot away to the safety of the reef below.

We escorted the woman to the back of the boat and helped her up onto the dive step at the stern. We were astonished at the damage caused by the small, young, normally placid fish. The inside of one of her thighs had been torn, and blood was flowing from ruptured veins. Fortunately, the fish had not bitten deep enough to slash through the femoral artery. That could have caused serious, even mortal, damage.

In January 2002 a report came in from Australia about two divers being harassed by a *six-foot-long,* several-hundred-pound grouper. It seemed intent on trying, at least, to eat them. It sneaked up on one diver and took his entire head in its mouth. Only quick, aggressive action by his buddy saved the diver from serious injury or worse.

I grew up knowing how violent and voracious bluefish could be during a feeding frenzy. Every summer I fished for them off Nantucket. When birds were working on a school of baitfish, and bluefish were attacking from below, the carnage was amazing. The blues would roll and leap and dive, snapping at everything with their scalpel-sharp triangular teeth.

From the safety of the boat, I never gave a thought to what would happen to a person who found himself in the water amid the feeding bluefish.

A lifeguard in Florida found out. He was sitting on a surfboard in calm water less than a hundred yards offshore.

First, flocks of gulls and terns drove a huge mass of baitfish toward him. Then he saw—he could tell from the sudden, roiling chop in the glass-calm sea and the glint of sunlight off the scales of rolling fish—that a school of blues was assaulting the baitfish.

He watched, spellbound, as the feeding frenzy came closer. He didn't move, didn't paddle away, just sat there with his feet dangling over the sides of the surfboard.

The bluefish struck so fast and their teeth were so sharp that two of the lifeguard's toes were gone before he could yank his feet out of the water.

In the newspaper account I read, the lifeguard didn't talk about the pain he felt. He didn't talk about what he had done to slow the flow of blood from his mangled foot while he paddled ashore. All that seemed to be on his mind was the terror he felt at the thought of a dozen frenzied bluefish flinging themselves onto his surfboard and continuing to chomp on him. Or the ultimate horror of what would happen if, through panic or clumsiness, he capsized his surfboard, fell into the water, and was eaten to death by a thousand ravenous fish.

Nature has spent millennia creating balanced ecosystems all over the world. On one island, there are just the right kind and number of snakes to keep the bird and rodent populations in check. On another, the proper plants nourish the resident animals, and the appropriate insects pollinate the plants.

Huge, isolated landmasses such as Australia contain several different kinds of environments—jungles, deserts, mountains, forests, and coastlines that vary from straight and sandy to cold and rocky to warm and swampy. In each environment different natural balances have evolved. Animals, plants, and insects live well together, feeding and sustaining one another.

The sudden introduction of new species—almost always by humans, intentionally or not—can, and usually does, disrupt those natural balances. Sometimes the disruptions are catastrophic to local populations. In the Galápagos Islands, for example, the introduction long ago of pigs and goats (from passing ships) destroyed populations of birds and reptiles that laid their eggs in the ground. And nowadays, tourist cruise boats inadvertently transport colonies of insects from one island to another. This creates chaos among resident plant and insect populations that have no defenses against the newcomers.

Some of the Hawaiian Islands have lost almost all their native birds to an invasion of voracious snakes from Guam. Scientists believe these snakes were stowaways in ships' cargoes and sometimes in the wheel wells of passenger jetliners across the Pacific.

The so-called killer bees from Africa were brought over to South America by scientists trying to create a productive new strain of bees. Inevitably, some of the bees escaped. Over the past several years they have gradually made their way north up the American continent. They have overpowered and crossbred with native species, creating ferociously aggressive new strains of ill-tempered bees.

Kudzu, an Asian plant, was imported into the American South. Because it has no natural predators there, it has overrun enormous areas of several states. Gypsy moths were imported into the American North by a well-meaning but wrongheaded scientist, and they've become a plague upon our trees.

Another instance of man attempting to manipulate nature put me and my family into one of the weirdest encounters of my life.

Wendy, Christopher, and I were in Moorea, the island forty minutes by fast boat across the Sea of the Moon from Tahiti. Christopher was ten, and this was the second year we had taken him with us to explore the waters of Polynesia while I did a story for a magazine. He was already an accomplished diver. Over the next couple of years he would become more experienced as he joined us on two voyages to explore the underwater world of the Galápagos.

Our hotel in Moorea featured a swim-with-the-dolphins attraction. I'm aware of the controversy surrounding human contact with captive marine animals, especially captive dolphins and whales. With a few specific exceptions, I'm against holding large marine animals in captivity.

Still, we decided to try this program. Christopher had never been in the water with a dolphin. Besides, the facility in Moorea was not a normal captive-interaction program. It seemed to me to be particularly enlightened. For one thing, the two trained dolphins were not captives. They had access to the open ocean and were free to come and go as they pleased. They had been conditioned only to return to the tank at the hotel twice each day. Then they would be fed and permitted—the trainer swore that they didn't have to be coaxed—to interact with a few humans.

Before we entered the tank, the trainer explained to us that the two dolphins were of an especially intelligent branch of the family *Delphinidae*. They were rough-toothed dolphins, a male and a female, each approximately eight feet long. They were not trained to do tricks. They would simply come to us when and as they chose and swim among us. We could extend our hands and feel the hard, slick skin as the dolphins passed, but we were not to grab a dorsal fin and hitch a ride or to try to hold the dolphins in any way.

The tank was approximately four feet deep and a hundred feet in diameter. When we were all in the water, the trainer signaled to his assistant, who opened the gate between the tank and an exterior holding pen.

Immediately the two dolphins swam into the tank. For a moment they paused together on the far side. I imagined they were like two performers facing a small audience and discussing how best to wow them. And then . . . well, first I'd better explain something:

At the moment when what happened was happening, I hadn't a clue as to what was really going on, or why. It took several days of talking to people who knew a great deal more about dolphins than I do before I understood how and why a macho-mad dolphin had threatened my life.

When the trainer told us that rough-toothed dolphins were smarter than most, he forgot to add that they're also temperamental and difficult. Other dolphin experts used words such as *cranky, aggressive,* and *darn well dangerous.*

While the male and female paused on the opposite side of the tank from where we were, they were studying us. Literally. Using their phenomenal sonar, they scanned our bodies, inside and out, and were able to determine our genders and our ages. Here's what they perceived: our party consisted of one male child (Christopher), one adult female (Wendy), and one adult male (me). To the male dolphin, Christopher was no threat. Wendy was a potential possession. I was—very definitely—a potential rival for its position as alpha male. I was to be gotten rid of, one way or another.

The dolphin's great intelligence was both the cause of my peril and my salvation. If its brain had been smaller, more primitive and less developed, it wouldn't have had the ability to perform such a detailed analysis of humans in its presence.

It also wouldn't have had the intelligence to choose between issuing a warning and launching an outright attack.

Why, I will never know—perhaps it took pity on me—but it decided to warn me, not kill me.

All I did know was this. From a dead stop, in what seemed like a fraction of a second, the bigger of the two dolphins crossed the tank. It passed between Christopher and Wendy without touching them. With a final, powerful thrust of its broad tail—which did wallop Wendy and leave her with a permanent dent in her thigh—it rammed me, at full speed, precisely between my legs.

It knew exactly what it was doing, what it was aiming to hit and what it was aiming to miss. It didn't want to injure, maim, or kill me. It certainly could have. (Dolphins can and do butt sharks to death frequently, and once in a great while they kill humans who tease or otherwise mess with them.) It wanted to warn me. It was saying, This is *my* turf, bub, and all females herein are mine, so *scram!*

The four- or five-hundred-pound dolphin was too big to pass between my legs. So when it struck me it lifted me high into the air, out of the water, and thrust me several feet away. I recall a weird sensation of having been hit by a torpedo, so hard and slick was its skin.

In a wink the dolphin zipped away, circled, and started back again. The trainer, who had watched the assault dumbstruck, came to life. He blew his whistle, waved his hands at the dolphin, and stepped between the dolphin and me.

The dolphin stopped so suddenly that it would have left rubber, had it had wheels.

"Get out!" the trainer shouted to us, over his shoulder. "Get out of the pool!"

We three waded to the edge of the tank and hoisted ourselves out of the water. Only then did Wendy feel the pain in her leg and see the deep purple crease in her thigh.

Christopher hadn't understood any of what had just happened. He was laughing himself silly. He thought the dolphin had been playing.

Me? I felt confused and slightly sick.

The trainer covered his embarrassment and surprise by sending the dolphin away with angry hand signals. He told us that nothing like this had ever happened before. Ever, ever, ever. He promised. And it would never happen again. He would teach the dolphin a lesson by punishing it. It wouldn't be allowed to play with any more humans for the rest of the day.

He said he hoped that I wouldn't need to mention the incident in the story I was writing. For—truly—never in all his years had anything like this happened before.

I said I saw no reason to publicize the episode. After all, no one had been seriously hurt, and this was a fluke.

The next day David Doubilet, who had been taking pictures on another island, arrived on Moorea. Without contacting us, he visited the same "dolphinarium."

The same dolphin did the same thing to him, driving him from the tank before he could snap a single picture.

It was tempting to lay all the blame on the operators of the facility. But I knew that, really, I had only myself to blame. I hadn't been savvy enough about this particular species of dolphin. And I had violated one of the fundamental rules of venturing into the sea. I had made my wife, young child, and myself vulnerable to the instincts of a large, strong, and—above all—*wild* oceanic predator.

We can be so eager to humanize all the world's animals that we forget to respect the most precious element in an animal's life: its wildness.

15
Okay, So What Can We Do?

On a beautiful autumn day in late March 1999, I knelt inside the belly cavity of a gargantuan great white shark and helped a scientist hunt for its heart.

In life, she had been nearly eighteen feet long—longer than all but the biggest SUVs—and had weighed nearly two tons. By now, after a year of being frozen, she had shrunk by a foot and had lost a few hundred pounds of water weight.

Still, the two of us fit easily within her. When the *National Geographic* cameraman approached for a close-up, there was plenty of room for him as well.

This huge beast had died, or been killed, or had killed herself by rolling up in a coastal longline set to catch big Australian snappers. She became trapped and finally asphyxiated. Like all sharks of her kind, she stayed alive only by constantly moving forward and flushing oxygen-rich water over her gills. Once trapped, she died from a lack of oxygen.

The fisherman who found her had towed her to shore and notified the authorities. Though it was illegal to kill a great white shark in the state of South Australia, this death had obviously been accidental, and no charges were lodged. In fact, the police were grateful to the fisherman. He could easily have cut the shark away from his line and let it sink to the bottom. When he asked for permission to keep the jaw, however, his request was denied. A great-white-shark jaw this huge might fetch ten thousand Australian dollars from a collector. News of such a sale might encourage other fishermen to discover other "accidental" catches.

The scientific community regretted that the enormous predator had died. But individual scientists were delighted to have the opportunity—very rare, indeed—to study a fully mature, intact, and undamaged female great white shark.

First, though, they had to find a freezer large enough to hold her until they could decide exactly what to do with her and how and where to do it. They located a gigantic cold box a few miles outside Adelaide. There they stowed this special specimen—until now.

I had been working for months on a story for *National Geographic* magazine and a television special for NGTV about great white sharks. The story was going to be published (and broadcast) in the spring of 2000, as close as possible to the twenty-fifth anniversary of the release of the movie version of *Jaws*. David Doubilet and I had proposed the story. It was David's job to gather photographs the likes of which had never before been taken. It was my job to collect all the new information about great whites that had accumulated in the quarter century since the film had burst upon the public consciousness.

John Bredar, the gifted producer/director of the television film, told me that the gigantic shark was about to be brought in from the cold, thawed, and studied. I quickly volunteered to return to the other side of the planet, where we had been diving with great whites only a couple of months earlier.

Thawing the shark took several days—well, hey, do you have a microwave capable of defrosting a thirty-five-hundred-pound fish? On the first day she was displayed, on a trailer bed at the South Australia Research and Development Institute (SARDI) outside the town of Glenelg, twelve thousand people showed up. They waited in line for hours, in a driving rain, for the chance to see, touch, feel, and smell the most formidable predator any of them had ever seen—or, probably, ever imagined.

She was magnificent even in death. Her length, her breadth, her sheer bulk struck spectators of every age dumb. They ran their fingers over the serrated sides of each of her inch-and-a-half-long upper teeth. Nobody said much, and those who did speak kept their voices low. I heard not one smart-mouth crack, not one lame joke. I knew that if someone had made even a mildly cynical remark, the crowd would have turned on him and shamed him into silence.

The folks were fascinated, yes, and awed. But as the hours passed and the crowd kept shuffling through, the sentiment I felt most strongly was reverence. What they were seeing was not merely a legend come true. It was tangible evidence of the power of nature.

The next day the shark was moved farther out of town, to the Bolivar Maceration Facility. This facility is a big, hangarlike building on open land, where whales and other large marine animals that washed up onshore were cut into disposable pieces.

Bolivar was where Dr. Barry Bruce, a famous SARDI biologist from Tasmania, and I would be filmed dissecting the great white shark. (Actually, of course, he would dissect and comment while I watched and asked questions.)

Bolivar stank. Oh, my, did it stink! Every square inch of every surface, every atom of air that flowed from the great gleaming tanks full of rotting flesh reeked. The smell was so nauseating that it brought tears to our eyes. I was given a chic yellow rubber apron to wear, along with striking black rubber boots and lovely pink rubber gloves. Still, the stink invaded every fiber of my cotton clothes. Eventually, after a few useless washings, I had to wrap them in plastic and put them out with the garbage.

The shark lay on her back. Her rigid dorsal fin forced her to be tilted slightly to the left. This shifted her massive insides leftward in a bulge that threatened to roll her off the dissecting table. Barry and his team of assistants and students had placed buckets and plastic vats all around the table to catch whatever fell out when the shark was opened up. Barry sharpened the twelve-inch blade of a carving knife. John Bredar placed me, his cameraman, his lights, and his sound equipment in perfect positions to announce and record any and all discoveries.

Nobody knew what we would find inside the shark. Nobody guessed aloud about the possibilities, though we all silently shared the same thoughts. *A keg of nails? Half a horse? A whole swordfish? A sea lion? A human leg? An entire person?* All of these and a thousand other unlikely objects had been found before inside great white sharks.

Barry placed the point of his knife against the belly of the beast. I cleared my throat. The cameraman said the magic word, *speed,* telling John that the camera was rolling at the proper rate. John gave Barry a quiet "Action!" and the dissection began.

Have you ever daydreamed about plunging your knife into the belly of an attacking shark? Perhaps you're diving down to open the treasure chest. Suddenly a dark shadow falls over you and the giant shark attacks. You duck below the monster and reach up with your knife hand. You slide the blade into the soft white flesh of the underbelly, splitting it open like a ripe melon and sending the mortally wounded shark off to die in the deep.

Well, forget it. Your knife would either bounce off or break off, and you'd face a future as lunch.

Barry struggled to slice through skin—no, *meat!*—more than an inch thick. He explained that female great whites are armored by nature to protect them during mating. It's a violent affair. The male repeatedly bites the female as he tries to keep his grip on her.

As the slit in the shark's belly grew longer, pressure increased from within, and cutting became quicker.

Someone said, "Watch out."

"For what?" I asked.

"The liver. It's a third of the body weight. Here it comes!"

And here, forcing its way out through the hole in the shark, came a thousand-pound liver. This immense organ of energy storage permitted the shark to go without eating for a month or more after one substantial meal.

For a couple of hours the dissection proceeded methodically. Barry described each of his findings. First he used layman's terms for the camera, then scientific jargon for the tape recorder monitored by one of his aides.

The shark's fins were sliced off. As each was tossed into a bin, we spoke of the sorry fact that there were people all over the world who would gladly have butchered this shark for her fins alone.

She bore old mating scars on her flanks, and her uterus was stretched (indicating that she had borne young). But she was not pregnant when she died.

We took breaks to change tapes and batteries and to rinse our lungs with fresh air. During one break I was taken on a hunt for Australia's notorious funnel web spider. Small (about the size of your thumbnail) and inoffensive-looking, Australian funnel webs are among the most poisonous spiders on the planet. Unfortunately, they are common in populated areas like suburbs. It took us less than five minutes to find several—in a woodpile, under old equipment, beside a corner of the building. This reinforced my belief that Australians are some of humanity's hardiest and most sensible people.

Wherever they live, travel, hike, swim, fish, dive, kayak, or trek, Australians risk being confronted by something capable of doing them in with tooth, fang, claw, jaw, or stinger. Yet there is no public outcry to get rid of any animal because it is dangerous to humans. Australians have learned to coexist in relative peace with nearly everything. When occasionally a human life is lost to an animal, the public's reaction is usually thoughtful and rational.

It was after noon when Barry decided that the time had come to open the shark's stomach and examine its contents. What would be in there? We all watched with great anticipation.

Barry slit the stomach sac, and following a flood of liquid, there came . . .

. . . not much, really, except confirmation of how the shark had died. The stomach contained three intact fifteen- or twenty-pound snappers, swallowed whole and complete with hooks, leaders, and lengths of line. There were a few bits and pieces of other prey: beaks from small squids and octopuses, otoliths (bony pieces from the inner ear) from different fish. A four-inch-long stingray barb, whose owner must have been eaten a long time before, had already moved through several inches of dense flesh on its way to rejection by the shark's amazingly rugged defense mechanisms.

We shared a feeling of letdown. Inside the shark there were no seals or walruses, whole or in part, no scientists, or politicians—not even a license plate or two.

By now, our excitement had been replaced by subdued silence. As Barry reached up behind the jaw and felt around for the shark's heart, we could see that the once magnificent creature had been reduced to little more than a memory. Only the head remained intact.

What I felt most, I think, was sorrow at the waste. The death of this giant had benefited no one. Maybe Barry and his team would come up with discoveries or conclusions that might help protect other sharks. Maybe the young people in the crowds that had stood in line to see the great white would grow up with respect and affection for the animals. I hoped so. Because otherwise, the result of this accidental catch and all the attention that came with it would be merely one less apex predator in the critical food chain at the bottom of the world.

Nature is very careful with her apex predators. They were not made with humans in mind. Remember, they've been present on earth, more or less exactly as they are today, for tens of millions of years. They cannot survive interference, accidental or intentional, from us.

At the rate at which great whites are being killed all over the world, the existence of certain populations is already threatened. The survival of the entire species may soon be in doubt.

Future generations may be able to know great white sharks only from film and videotape.

The same is true, to a greater or lesser degree, of other sharks and other fish.

The fact is that every major fishery in the world is being overexploited, pushed beyond its capacities. At a time when a swelling human population needs more animal protein than ever, catches of almost every important food fish are in decline.

Everywhere, too many fishermen with too much sophisticated gear are chasing too few fish.

This problem can be solved only by us, and only if we will reexamine our place in nature and rethink our conduct as members of the natural order.

We are only one among millions of species of animals. We—that is, humankind—have long assumed that we are superior to all the others and that they exist only to serve our needs, our wants, our pleasures.

Wrong!

They are our equals as tenants of this fragile planet. Nature created each one to serve a purpose, to fill a place in the grand scheme of life on earth. It is not up to us to decide what will die and what will live. Nor do we have the right to conduct our lives so carelessly that we destroy others by accident.

Each and every animal deserves our respect and concern as we share our journey.

GLOSSARY

AFT: near or toward the rear of a boat.

AMPULLAE OF LORENZINI: bundles of sensory cells connected to nerve fibers in the head of a shark that allow it to detect electric fields.

ANTHROPOMORPHIZE: to use human characteristics to describe nonhuman things.

APEX PREDATOR: an animal at the top of the food chain.

THE BENDS: (also called decompression sickness) pain and other symptoms caused by leaving a compressed atmosphere too quickly. Bends can be fatal.

BIOLUMINESCENCE: light produced by living organisms.

BOW: the front of a boat.

BRACKISH: salty, dirty. Brackish water is often found where a river meets the sea.

BUOY: an anchored float used to mark a reef or channel, or to moor a boat.

CARNIVORE: a meat-eating animal.

CARTILAGE: a tough, elastic connective tissue. It is found in humans in various parts of the body, such as the ear, nose, and throat, and forms a shark's skeleton.

CAUDAL KEEL: the horizontal ridges along the tail fin of sharks and other fast-swimming fish.

CETACEAN: a marine mammal in the order (Cetacea) that includes whales, dolphins, and porpoises.

CHITIN: a horny substance that forms part of that hard outer layer of crustaceans and insects.

CHUM: chopped fish or other organic matter used as bait.

CLEAT: a T-shaped piece of metal or wood on a boat, to which ropes are attached.

CRUSTACEAN: one of a large group of aquatic animals with shells that includes lobsters, shrimp, and crabs.

DERMAL DENTICLES: tiny scalelike teeth that make up the skin of a shark.

DORSAL FIN: a fin on the back of a fish or marine mammal, such as the tall triangular one on a shark or a killer whale.

ELASMOBRANCH: a class of fish with a skeleton made of cartilage (not bone), including sharks, rays, and skates.

EMBOLUS: an air bubble or clot that has been carried through the bloodstream to block an artery.

FLANK: the side of the body, between the ribs and hip, on animals and humans.

FLOTSAM: floating wreckage of a ship or its cargo.

NICTITATING MEMBRANE: an inner eyelid that closes to protect the eye of birds, reptiles, and many sharks.

PECTORAL FIN: each of a pair of fins on either side just behind a fish's head.

PLANKTON: tiny plants and animals that serve as food for larger fish.

PORT: the left side of a boat (when you are facing forward).

PREDATION: obtaining food by killing and eating animals.

REEF: a chain of rocks or coral at or near the surface of the sea.

REGULATOR: a device that controls the pressure from a tank of compressed air, allowing a diver to breathe comfortably underwater.

SANDBAR: a ridge of sand built up by currents.

SCAVENGER: an animal that feeds on dead or decaying matter.

SHOAL: a sandbank or sandbar that makes the water shallow.

STARBOARD: the right side of a boat (when you are facing forward).

STERN: the rear end of a boat.

SYMBIOSIS: the close association of two different organisms living together in a mutually beneficial relationship.

TOURNIQUET: a device, such as a tight bandage, used to stop bleeding.

WET SUIT: a tight-fitting rubber suit worn for warmth in water sports or diving.

For more information about sharks and shark attacks and for directions to further educational sites and materials, visit the Shark Research Institute at www.sharks.org. For information on conservation efforts and how you can help, I recommend a group called WildAid at www.wildaid.org.

About the author

Peter Benchley is the bestselling author of *Jaws, The Deep,* and *Beast,* among others. His articles and essays have appeared in many publications, including *National Geographic* and the *New York Times.* He has written screenplays for the movie versions of three of his novels and has written, narrated, and appeared in dozens of television documentaries. Peter Benchley is a member of the National Council for Environmental Defense and a spokesman for its Oceans Program.